LITERATURE C
SOURC

Jubilee

and Related Readings

McDougal Littell
A HOUGHTON MIFFLIN COMPANY
Evanston, Illinois • Boston • Dallas

Links to *The Language of Literature*

If you are using *Jubilee* in connection with *The Language of Literature,* please note that thematic connections can be easily made between the novel and the following units:

- Grade 11, Unit 4: Conflict and Expansion, 1850–1900
- Grade 11, Unit 5: The Changing Face of America, 1855–1925

Acknowledgments

Page 8: Excerpts from *How I Wrote Jubilee* by Margaret Walker. Copyright © 1972 by Margaret Walker. Reprinted by permission of Third World Press, Inc., Chicago, Illinois.

ISBN 0-395-87487-4

1234567—MAL—03 02 01 00 99 98 97

Table of Contents

Into the Literature: *Creating Context*

Through the Literature: *Developing Understanding*

Beyond the Literature: *Synthesizing Ideas*

Parts of the SourceBook

- **Table of Contents**
- **Overview Chart**
- **Summaries of the Literature**
- **Customizing Instruction**

Into the Literature
CREATING CONTEXT

- **Cultural/Historical/Author Background**
- **Critic's Corner** Excerpts from literary criticism about *Jubilee*
- **Literary Concepts**
- **Motivating Activities**

Through the Literature
DEVELOPING UNDERSTANDING

- **Discussion Starters** Questions for the class to respond to orally after reading each section, including a Literary Concept question and a Writing Prompt
- **FYI Pages for Students** Reproducible masters that offer students background, vocabulary help, and connections to the modern world as they read the literature
- **FYI Glossary** Reproducible glossary of difficult words from each section of *Jubilee*
- **Strategic Reading worksheets** Reproducible masters to help students keep track of the plot as they read (Literal and inferential reading)
- **Literary Concept worksheets** Reproducible masters to help students understand the use of literary elements (Critical reading)
- **Vocabulary worksheet** Reproducible master to help students learn essential vocabulary used in the novel

Beyond the Literature
SYNTHESIZING IDEAS

- **Culminating Writing Assignments** Exploratory, research, and literary analysis topics for writing, covering both the main work and the related readings
- **Multimodal Activities** Suggestions for short-term projects, some of which are cross-curricular
- **Cross-Curricular Projects** Suggestions for long-term, cross-curricular, cooperative learning projects
- **Suggestions for Assessment**
- **Test, Answer Key** Essay and short-answer test on *Jubilee* and the related readings, with answer key
- **Additional Resources** Additional readings for students (coded by difficulty level) and teachers, as well as bibliographic information about commercially available technology

	PAGES FOR TEACHER'S USE	PAGES FOR STUDENT'S USE
Literature Connections	**SourceBook**	**Reproducible Pages**
Jubilee	Customizing Instruction, p. 5; Into the Literature: Creating Context, pp. 6–8; Critic's Corner, pp. 9–11; Literary Concepts: Historical Novel, Point of View, Structure, pp. 12–14; Motivating Activities, p. 15	**FYI, p. 27** **Glossary, pp. 39–40** **Vocabulary, p. 47**
Jubilee Part I, pp. 3–188	Discussion Starters, p. 16	**FYI, pp. 28–29; Glossary, p. 39** **Strategic Reading 1, p. 41** **Literary Concept 1, p. 44**
Jubilee Part II, pp. 189–338	Discussion Starters, p. 17	**FYI, pp. 30–31** **Glossary, pp. 39–40** **Strategic Reading 2, p. 42**
Jubilee Part III, pp. 339–536	Discussion Starters, p. 18	**FYI, pp. 32–33; Glossary, p. 40** **Strategic Reading 3, p. 43** **Literary Concepts 2, 3, pp. 45, 46**
"Virginia Portrait," pp. 543–545	Discussion Starters, p. 19	
from *Incidents in the Life of a Slave Girl,* pp. 546–559	Discussion Starters, p. 20	**FYI, p. 34**
"Raise a Ruckus Tonight" and "Many Thousand Gone," pp. 560–562	Discussion Starters, p. 21	**FYI, p. 35**
"Come Up from the Fields Father," pp. 563–565	Discussion Starters, p. 22	**FYI, p. 36**
"The Sheriff's Children," pp. 566–588	Discussion Starters, p. 23	**FYI, p. 37**
"Traveling the Long Road to Freedom," pp. 589–604	Discussion Starters, p. 24	**FYI, p. 38**
"To the University of Cambridge, in New-England," pp. 605–606	Discussion Starters, p. 25	
"To Phillis Wheatley," pp. 607–616	Discussion Starters, p. 25	
	Culminating Writing Assignments, p. 48; Multimodal Activities, pp. 49–50; Cross-Curricular Projects, pp. 51–54; Suggestions for Assessment, p. 55; Test, Answer Keys, pp. 58–59; Additional Resources, pp. 60–62	

Additional writing support for students can be found in the **Writing Coach.**

Jubilee
by Margaret Walker

Jubilee is a historical novel about Vyry, who is born into slavery on a plantation in southern Georgia but dreams of being free with a house of her own and seeing her children educated. When Vyry's lover, Randall Ware, escapes to the North but fails to return after the Civil War, Vyry marries Innis Brown, and with her children they set out for Alabama. The family endures a flood, a cruel landlord, and the Ku Klux Klan but finally get a farm and a home of their own. Vyry's son Jim grows restless, but eventually his father, Randall Ware, reappears. Vyry decides to stay with Innis but sees Jim go off happily with Ware to attend school. Vyry has lived to see all her dreams fulfilled.

RELATED READINGS

Virginia Portrait
by Sterling A. Brown

For the woman in this poem, a serene winter arrives at last.

from Incidents in the Life of a Slave Girl
by Harriet A. Jacobs

Harriet Jacobs escaped from her owners, hid for nearly seven years, then fled north in 1842. Still in danger, she was bought by friends and freed in 1852. Her autobiography describes experiences that parallel Vyry's.

Raise a Ruckus Tonight and Many Thousand Gone
Traditional

The first song tells of promises broken. The second is a reaction to emancipation.

Come Up from the Fields Father
by Walt Whitman

Whitman's poem captures the emotions of those on the home front who wait for their men to come back from the Civil War.

The Sheriff's Children
by Charles Waddell Chesnutt

In this story, Charles Waddell Chesnutt shows a devastating consequence of the color line in post–Civil War America.

Traveling the Long Road to Freedom
by Donovan Webster

This article tells how an African-American historian followed the footsteps of slaves escaping on the Underground Railroad 150 years ago.

To the University of Cambridge, in New-England
by Phillis Wheatley

Phillis Wheatley founded the African-American literary tradition. Here she offers advice to the Harvard students of her time.

To Phillis Wheatley
by Lisa Clayton

A young Harvard woman in the 1990s thinks about her ties with Wheatley and poses questions she would like to ask her if she could.

Customizing Instruction

Less Proficient Readers

- Before students begin to read, help them understand that *Jubilee* is a work of fiction that contains historical details. Explain that Walker interweaves fictional characters and events with real people and actual events from history.

- To help students grasp the novel's historical context, have them discuss what they know about slavery in the United States and about the Civil War. Direct their attention to the background information, and suggest that they read more about these subjects in their American history textbooks or in other history books. You may also want to show one of the films listed in **Additional Resources,** page 62.

- Some students will have difficulty with the scope of *Jubilee.* To help them keep track of characters and key events, suggest that they make a chart listing characters' names, their relationships to one another, and what happens to them during the course of the novel.

- Students who need help with the literal comprehension of the plot may use copies of **Strategic Reading 1–3** worksheets, pages 41–43, as they read.

- Ask students to learn the 25 asterisked words in the **Glossary,** pages 39–40. Review these words in class, and have students practice using them orally or in written paragraphs. They may also make word webs, based on words relating to slavery, to show relationships between words and themes.

Students Acquiring English

- To help students understand where events in *Jubilee* take place, use a map of the United States to identify states in the South. Mention that the novel is set in Georgia and Alabama, and point out the states that seceded from the Union to form the Confederate States of America—Virginia, North Carolina, South Carolina, Georgia, Texas, Florida, Alabama, Mississippi, Louisiana, Arkansas, and Tennessee.

- Students may have difficulty with the use of dialect in this novel. Explain that dialect is a variation of a language spoken by the people of a particular region or group. Ask students to identify examples of dialect in their own experience. To help them hear Walker's dialect in *Jubilee,* read excerpts of dialogue aloud.

- If appropriate, use the suggestions listed above for Less Proficient Readers.

Gifted and Talented Students

- Have students create a time line of historical events as they read *Jubilee.* After they finish reading the novel, encourage them to research these events to find out more about what happened.

- Have students read another Civil War-era novel, such as *Gone with the Wind* by Margaret Mitchell. Have them compare and contrast this novel with *Jubilee.*

Into the Literature
CREATING CONTEXT

Jubilee

Jubilee was first published in 1966, more than 30 years after Margaret Walker began to write the novel. An international bestseller, *Jubilee* has never gone out of print, and millions of copies have been sold.

Although the novel received mixed reviews when it was published, *Jubilee* has been recognized as an important literary work because it is the first major historical novel written by an African American that tells the story of slavery and emancipation primarily as seen by African-American characters. According to Dr. Maryemma Graham, "Walker's revisionist account of the Civil War and the period of Reconstruction established a new tradition in southern American literature."

In addition to being a historical novel, *Jubilee* is considered to be a **neoslave narrative:** it combines elements from a factual slave narrative, drawn from the oral history of Walker's own family, with elements from African-American folklore and fiction. Walker uses this hybrid form not only to expose racism but to celebrate the faith and spirit of African Americans who endured the unimaginable injustices of slavery and the betrayals of Reconstruction.

The South in the 1800s

Jubilee is set in Georgia and Alabama in the 1800s. The novel is divided into three parts, each covering a distinct time period: the antebellum Old South (1815–1860), the Civil War (1861–1865), and Reconstruction (1865–1877). Walker's chronological narrative, written from the perspective of an enslaved woman named Vyry, offers a glimpse of everyday life as it was lived by both blacks and whites.

The Original Vyry and Randall Ware

Although Vyry and Randall Ware in *Jubilee* are fictional characters, they are modeled on Walker's maternal great-grandparents, Margaret Duggans Ware Brown and Randall Ware. Walker gathered details about her great-grandparents through the stories that her grandmother, Elvira Ware Dozier—the character Minna in the novel—told her, through conversations with her grandmother's youngest sister, and through research. Like their counterparts in the novel, Margaret Brown was a plantation slave and Ware was an educated, prosperous free African American who worked as a blacksmith in Dawson, Georgia.

> **Note:** Since this novel deals realistically with issues of slavery and racial oppression, offensive terms such as "nigger" and "nigra" are frequently spoken by some of the characters. You may wish to discuss this issue with students before they begin reading.

Walker's Life

1915 Born July 7 in Birmingham, Alabama, the daughter of a Methodist minister and a music teacher.

1927 Begins to write poetry and details of her grandmother's slavery stories in a writer's journal that her father gave to her.

1931 Meets Langston Hughes, a poet associated with the Harlem Renaissance, at New Orleans University. Hughes encourages Walker to write and to receive formal training.

1934 "Daydreaming," later retitled "I Want to Write," appears in *The Crisis* magazine. Begins to write the first draft of *Jubilee*.

1935 Receives a bachelor's degree in English from Northwestern University. After graduating, she joins the Federal Writers' Project in Chicago and meets the African-American writers Arna Bontemps, Gwendolyn Brooks, and Richard Wright.

1940 Receives a master's degree in creative writing from the University of Iowa.

1942 Becomes the first African-American writer to win the Yale Series of Younger Poets Award for her first volume of poetry, *For My People*.

1943 Marries Firnist James Alexander.

1949 Takes a position as a professor of English at Jackson State College in Jackson, Mississippi, where she teaches for 26 years.

1954 Wins the Ford Fellowship for study at Yale University.

1965 Earns a doctorate from the University of Iowa.

1966 Publishes *Jubilee* and wins the Houghton Mifflin Literary Fellowship.

1968 Establishes the Institute for the Study of the History, Life and Culture of Black People, which in 1989 is renamed the Margaret Walker Alexander National African American Research Center.

1970 Publishes *Prophets for a New Day,* a collection of poems about civil rights leaders.

1979 Retires from Jackson State College to pursue her career as a writer, public speaker, and community leader.

1988 Publishes *Richard Wright: Daemonic Genius,* a biography of her friend.

1989 Publishes *This Is My Century: New and Collected Poems*.

1990s Begins a sequel to *Jubilee,* tentatively titled *Minna and Jim,* and begins writing her autobiography.

Walker on Walker

On her grandmother's slavery stories—

"When my great-grandmother—Vyry in the story—died, a month before I was born, in 1915, grandmother was already in Birmingham waiting with my mother for my birth. Since my grandmother lived with us until I was an adult, it was natural throughout my formative years for me to hear stories of slave life in Georgia. We moved from Birmingham to New Orleans when I was a small child, and my mother recalls how often she and my father came in from night school well past bedtime and found me enthralled in my grandmother's stories. Annoyed, she would ask, 'Mama, why won't you let that child go to bed? Why will you keep her up until this time of night?' And grand-mother usually answered guiltily, 'Go to bed, Margaret. Go to bed right now.' My father would add, 'Telling her all those harrowing tales, just nothing but tall tales.' Grandma grew indignant then, saying, 'I'm not telling her tales; I'm telling her the naked truth.'

As I grew older and realized the importance of the story my grand-mother was telling, I prodded her with more questions: 'What hap-pened after the war, Grandma? Where did they go? Where did they live after that place?' I was already conceiving the story of *Jubilee* vaguely, and early in my adolescence, while I was still hearing my grandmother tell old slavery-time stories and incidents from her mother's life, I promised my grandmother that when I grew up I would write her mother's story. I'm sorry she did not live to see the book."

QUOTED IN *HOW I WROTE* JUBILEE *AND OTHER ESSAYS ON LIFE AND LITERATURE*

On the historical underpinnings of *Jubilee*—

"I told myself that I must surely be ready to write the story now. . . . My family story could cover five generations of Negroes living in the South. I had a superstructure of facts assembled from word-of-mouth accounts, slave narratives, history books, documents, newspapers; and now I had only to give my material the feel of a fabric of life. At this point I seemed to have a vision of the whole artistic task before me—the creation of fiction from fact, the development of imagined clothing, of muscle and flesh for the real and living bones of history. . . .

How much of *Jubilee* is fiction and how much fact? When you have lived with a story as long as I have with this one, it is difficult sometimes to separate the two, but let us say that the basic skeleton of the story is factually true and authentic. Imagination has worked with this factual material, however, for a very long time. The entire story follows a plot line of historical incidents from the first chapter until the last: the jour-neys, the Big Road, the violence, the battles, the places Vyry and Innis lived and the reasons they moved."

QUOTED IN *HOW I WROTE* JUBILEE *AND OTHER ESSAYS ON LIFE AND LITERATURE*

Critic's Corner

ABRAHAM CHAPMAN

Chapman, Abraham. Review of *Jubilee.*
***Saturday Review,* September 24, 1966.**

To appreciate the extent of innovation *Jubilee* brings to a thoroughly quarried, frequently hackneyed genre of writing, it is only necessary to recall that the Civil War novel has been the source of some of the crudest stereotypes of Negro characters in American fiction. . . . Margaret Walker has reversed the picture completely. With a fidelity to fact and detail, she presents the little-known everyday life of the slaves, their modes of behavior, patterns and rhythms of speech, emotions, frustrations, and aspirations. Never done on such a scale before, this is the strength of her novel. As it unfolds one sees plantation life as it was seen by Negro slaves, feels the texture of American history as it was felt by Negro slaves: the Civil War with the hopes it aroused, its sordid and grim realities; the participation of the Negroes in the fight against slavery; the ugly and frustrating rise of the Ku Klux Klan; the postwar waves of terror in the South to keep the Negro down and prevent emancipation from becoming a reality.

The author is so intent on presenting her historical data as accurately as possible, or correcting the distortions which have crept into so many Civil War novels, that at times she fails to transform her raw material into accomplished literary form. There are passages of very pedestrian prose. Fortunately, the colorful and musical speech of the Negro characters in the novel transcends the stilted prose of the narrator.

WILMA DYKEMAN

Dykeman, Wilma. Review of *Jubilee. New York Times Book Review,* September 25, 1966.

[This is an] ambitious and uneven novel. . . . Several of its major characters . . . emerge as stereotypes. Some scenes remain less than fully realized, more catalogued than rendered. . . . [The publishers state that this] "is told from the Negro point of view by a Negro." What is of first importance in a novel is not the race of the author or the sources of its inspiration but its ring of artistic truth. . . . In its best episodes, and in Vyry, *Jubilee* chronicles the triumph of a free spirit over many kinds of bondages.

Critic's Corner

GUY DAVENPORT

Davenport, Guy. Review of *Jubilee*. *National Review*, October 4, 1966.

The dialects are fake [and] the novel from end to end is about a place and a people who never existed. . . . But if you want to go strolling through the myth again, here it is, nothing left out: darkies singing out beyond the watermelon patch, the cruel overseer, the frigid wife, the handsome son, the underground railway, the War, Reconstruction— even a plot of sorts. . . . There is something deeply ironic in a Negro's underwriting the . . . South of the romancers, agreeing to every convention of the trade. . . . Slavery was far stranger and more terrible than the myth that Miss Walker has swallowed.

ELEANOR TRAYLOR

Traylor, Eleanor. "Music as Theme: The Blues Mode in the Works of Margaret Walker." *Black Women Writers (1950–1980): A Critical Evaluation.* Ed. Mari Evans. Garden City, NY: Anchor Books, 1984.

Music is the leitmotif of Margaret Walker's *Jubilee*. The celebrant of the novel is a singer. Her songs articulate progressive stages in her life; they amplify its meaning. Through her songs, the personal history of Vyry, Elvira Ware Brown, central dramatic figure, actual maternal great-grandmother of the author, merges with the history of a community, of a time, of a place, of a space—a mythical zone—within the history of world story. Vyry, "adrift," as in "a wide world alone," is a unique wayfarer whose journey, as charted in the bluesman's song, is a series of new beginnings. Her rhythmic movement through experience is not the movement of the ritual tragic hero: she does not topple from the heights of a social order and die in affirmation of a value. Nor does she muddle through the comic hero's bumbling acquiescence to the social norm. Hers is not the movement of the epic conqueror who requires, is general of, an army. She cannot rid the land of the corruption of the fruitful. Elvira's is no sentimental journey, no romance. . . . Her movement through time is a continuous process of dissolution, absorption, conversion, and realignment. She locates within her personal experience the public experience of the tribe. She harnesses the dislocations, the rifts, the shards of experience, and makes of them a whole appropriate to the moment.

Critic's Corner

BERNARD W. BELL

Bell, Bernard W. *The Afro-American Novel and Its Tradition.* Amherst, MA: The University of Massachusetts Press, 1987.

If it is the function of good realistic art to create character types of general appeal, then *Jubilee* is an impressive novel. In the creation of Vyry, Margaret Walker has given us one of the most memorable women in contemporary Afro-American fiction. A pillar of Christian faith and human dignity, Vyry, the protagonist of the novel, commands our respect first as an individual and then as a symbol of nineteenth-century black womanhood. Shaped by plantation culture, she realistically embodies its strengths and weaknesses. As John Dutton's illegitimate daughter, she could pass as the twin of her master's legitimate daughter, Lillian—"same sandy hair, same gray-blue eyes, same milk-white skin." She has thus a privileged yet precarious status in the caste system of the plantation. Raised in the Quarters of the Big House as a cook, she is neither bitter nor political in her philosophy of life. Her major strengths are integrity, resourcefulness, pragmatism, and songs. Her weaknesses are caste prejudice, fidelity to former white owners, and political naïveté. Torn between loyalty to her first husband and her white family, and loyalty to her second husband and her children, she is guided by her Christian ethics in arriving at a practical rather than radical resolution of the conflict. In contrast to the stereotypic loyal family retainer, she remains on the Dutton plantation after the war because of her promise to Randall Ware that she would wait for him and because of her compassion for her former white mistress. Expanding in the denouement of the novel on the significance of Vyry's character and culture, the author-narrator reveals a close moral and political identification with the protagonist and implicitly invites our similar response. . . . Vyry thus evolves as a heroic symbol of the black woman whose Christian faith, humanism, courage, resourcefulness, and music are the bedrock of her survival and the survival of her people. But by limiting Vyry's politics to the domestic and familial, Walker's vision celebrates the black woman of yesterday rather than of tomorrow.

Literary Concept
HISTORICAL NOVEL

Professor Joyce Anne Joyce called *Jubilee* "the first truly historical black American novel." A **historical novel** is one in which the events take place during a specific historical period. Typically, a historical novel does some or all of the following.

- It accurately depicts the customs, events, and attitudes of a particular historical period.
- It mixes fact and fiction.
- It explores social conflicts and how those conflicts personally affect one or more characters.
- It presents a historical conflict whose outcome is already known to the reader.
- It includes characters who are based on real people in history.

In *Jubilee,* Walker brings to life people, places, and events that are associated with the period before, during, and after the Civil War (1861–1865) in the United States. Against the backdrop of the 19th-century Deep South, Walker explores what happens to fictional characters such as Vyry, an enslaved African-American woman, during the antebellum period (the years before the war), during the war itself, and during Reconstruction, the postwar period in which the Confederate states were gradually readmitted to the Union.

Presentation Suggestions Remind students that a **historical novel** is a novel that attempts to reflect accurately the events and people of a particular historical period. If you wish to have students discuss the South of the 1800s before they begin to read *Jubilee,* have them hold an informal panel discussion to share their knowledge of slavery, the Civil War, and Reconstruction. You may suggest that as students read the novel, they list specific details related to the period, including the clothing people wore, the food they ate, the occupations they held, the social customs they followed, the attitudes they expressed, and the political and historical events they witnessed. After students have finished reading the novel, they may summarize in a three-column chart what they learned about life in the South before, during, and after the Civil War.

Distribute **Literary Concept 1** worksheet, page 44, to help students explore the characteristics of historical fiction.

Literary Concept
POINT OF VIEW

Point of view is the narrative perspective a writer uses to tell a story; that is, the vantage point from which the action is seen. Three different types of point of view are described in the following chart:

First-Person Point of View	Third-Person Limited Point of View	Third–Person Omniscient Point of View
Narrator is a character in the work, telling the story in his or her own words.	Narrator stands outside the action and focuses on one character's thoughts, observations, and feelings.	Narrator is an all-knowing, objective observer who stands outside the action, able to move about in time and place.
Reader sees only into narrator's mind.	Reader sees only into that character's mind.	Reader sees into various characters' minds.
Narrator uses first-person pronouns (I, me, my) in telling the story.	Narrator uses third-person pronouns (he, she, they) in telling the story.	Narrator uses third-person pronouns (he, she, they) in telling the story.

Jubilee is told from the third-person omniscient point of view. By using this narrative perspective, Walker is able to draw effective comparisons between the lives of the slaves and the lives of the wealthy slave owners, and to give readers deep insight into the thoughts and feelings of both white and black characters, whose lives are turned upside down by the Civil War.

Presentation Suggestions Remind students that **point of view** is the narrative perspective from which a story is told. To help students explore point of view after they read the novel, distribute **Literary Concept 2** worksheet, page 45. You may also want to ask them to rewrite a passage from *Jubilee* so that it is told from a different point of view. For example, they might use first-person point of view, telling what happens through either Vyry's or John Dutton's eyes. Encourage students to share their rewritten passages and to discuss how the story changes when told from a different point of view.

Literary Concept
STRUCTURE

The **structure** of a work of literature is the way the work is organized—that is, its planned framework. Walker divides *Jubilee* into three distinct parts, as shown below.

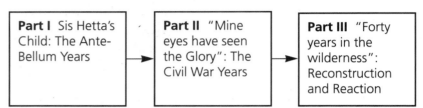

| **Part I** Sis Hetta's Child: The Ante-Bellum Years | **Part II** "Mine eyes have seen the Glory": The Civil War Years | **Part III** "Forty years in the wilderness": Reconstruction and Reaction |

Each part of the novel covers a different historical period and relates the events in Vyry's life that take place during that period. The first part of the novel deals with events that occur in Georgia in the years before the Civil War, the second part focuses on events that happen during the war, and the last part covers the turbulent social, political, and economic changes that take place after the war.

Presentation Suggestions Remind students that the **structure** of a work of literature is the way in which it is put together. To help them appreciate the chronological structure of *Jubilee,* you might have them create a graphic organizer, such as a flow chart or a time line, to record historical events that take place in each part of the book. Then ask students the following questions: Why do you think Walker structured the novel in three separate parts? What does the structure emphasize in the novel? What is the significance of the titles of the parts? How does the structure of the novel help to emphasize the impact of history on individuals? The **Literary Concept 3** worksheet, page 46, can be used to help students explore the structure of *Jubilee.*

Motivating Activities

1. **Concept Web** Have students work independently or in small groups to create a word web or other graphic organizer that explores one or more of these concepts: *slavery, oppression, prejudice, freedom.* Encourage students who are having trouble getting started to (1) define the concept, perhaps using a dictionary or a thesaurus; (2) give examples from their own experience or from their reading that illustrate the concept; and (3) list their personal reactions to and associations with the concept.

2. **Role-Playing** Prejudice, discrimination, and freedom from oppression are central themes in *Jubilee.* Have students explore these powerful concepts by role-playing or discussing one of the situations that follow.

   • Have you ever been treated unfairly because of race, religion, gender, social or economic status, or the way you look or dress? How did you personally respond? Do you think that your response was an appropriate one? Why or why not?

   • Think of people you have read about who successfully overcame oppression. For example, you might recall that Pilgrims migrated to America in pursuit of religious freedom and that Frederick Douglass became a prominent leader in the antislavery movement after he escaped from slavery. What kinds of oppression—economic, social, cultural, religious—do people experience? What steps can people take to fight oppression? What qualities or traits do you think might help or hinder someone who is fighting against oppression?

3. **Tapping Prior Knowledge: The Civil War** Invite students to work together as a class or in small groups to share what they know about the Civil War, including the causes and effects of the war, important battle sites, military strengths and weaknesses of the Confederate and Union armies, prominent military leaders, the role of African Americans and women in the war, and so forth. Record the students' facts and impressions on the board, to be used as a reference as they work through Part II of the novel and the accompanying activities.

4. **Linking to Today: Prejudice** Help students explore their views by asking volunteers to cite examples of prejudice that have recently been reported in a newspaper or on the TV news. As students discuss the examples, encourage them to think about different factors that contribute to prejudice as well as the negative effects of prejudice. Conclude by suggesting that students compare and contrast examples of prejudice in *Jubilee* with the real-life examples they have identified.

5. **FYI Background** Reproduce and distribute to students **FYI** page 27, which gives background information on *Jubilee.* You might reproduce and distribute all the **FYI** pages for the novel at this time, so that students can refer to them as they read.

Through the Literature

DEVELOPING UNDERSTANDING

BEFORE READING

You might want to distribute

 pp. 27–29; Glossary, p. 39
- *Strategic Reading 1, p. 41*
- *Literary Concept 1, p. 44*

Jubilee

PART I

Chapters 1—18

AFTER READING

Discussion Starters

1. What are your impressions of the antebellum years in the South after reading Part I? Jot down a few words or phrases.

2. When she is seven years old, Vyry is sent to the Big House. Do you think her life improves after she leaves the Quarters? Why or why not?

3. What qualities or traits do you think help Vyry to cope successfully with her day-to-day existence at Shady Oaks?

4. How would you describe John Morris Dutton?

CONSIDER
- ✓ his feelings for Hetta
- ✓ his marriage to Salina
- ✓ his relationship with his children
- ✓ his political aspirations
- ✓ his economic and social status

5. **Literary Concept: Historical Novel** List three details that help you visualize the time period in which Part I is set.

6. **Making Connections** From the 1700s through the Civil War, most African Americans in the South were, like Vyry, forced to live as slaves and subjected to the desires and demands of their white owners. What other group or groups of people in the United States do you think were treated unfairly in the past?

Writing Prompt

The first part of the novel takes place on John Dutton's plantation. Write a short **description** of Shady Oaks for a 19th-century travel guide, describing where it is located, who lives there, what the landscape is like, what plants and animals are found there, and other details.

BEFORE READING

You might want to distribute

 pp. 30–31; Glossary, pp. 39–40

• *Strategic Reading 2, p. 42*
• *Literary Concept 2, p. 45*

AFTER READING

Discussion Starters

1. What events in Part II did you find most moving or striking?
2. How would you describe the impact of the Civil War on the Duttons?

> ### CONSIDER
>
> ✓ the political, economic, and social changes that take place in the South during the war
>
> ✓ the losses suffered by the Duttons
>
> ✓ the psychological toll of the war on different family members

3. **Literary Concept: Point of View** How do you think the handling of point of view in Part II affects the reader's feelings about the Duttons?
4. What is your opinion of the roles that the African-American characters play in the Civil War?
5. What do you think motivates Vyry to stay on at the plantation after the war?
6. **Making Connections** Conflict between the North and the South over the issue of slavery sparked the Civil War in the 19th century. What divisive social or political conflicts do you think might appear in a historical novel set in the 20th century?

Writing Prompt

Choose a character who serves in the war, such as Johnny Dutton or Randall Ware. From the point of view of this character, write a **letter** home about your experiences.

You might want to distribute

 pp. 32–33; Glossary, p. 40
- *Strategic Reading 3, p. 43*
- *Literary Concept 3, p. 46*

PART III

Chapters 41—58

AFTER READING

Discussion Starters

1. What do you think about the ending of the novel?

2. **Literary Concept: Historical Novel** Which postwar problems that Vyry and her family experience do you think had the most negative impact on their lives? Explain.

3. What qualities or traits do you think helped Vyry and her family overcome the problems they encountered?

4. Do you think Vyry makes the right decision to stay with Innis Brown? Why or why not?

CONSIDER

✓ her feelings for Innis and the life she has built with him

✓ her feelings for Randall Ware and the life she might build with him

✓ her values and beliefs

✓ the welfare of her children

5. **Making Connections** In Part III, Mrs. Jacobson claims that Vyry and other freed slaves don't want to work hard, saying, "You expect everything to come dropping in your laps, houses and land and schools and churches and money." On the contrary, Vyry and her family struggle to begin their new lives with little outside help or support. Where can a person in need today turn for assistance? Think about different resources that are available, such as specific charitable organizations, government programs, social service agencies, and religious groups.

Writing Prompt

Consider Vyry's negative and positive experiences after she gains her freedom. Then write a **definition** of freedom based on her point of view. Complete the following sentence: Freedom is _____.

Virginia Portrait

Discussion Starters

1. What do you think of the woman in this poem? Describe her in a few words.
2. How would you describe the woman's feelings about death?
3. Which "simple joys" described in the fifth stanza do you share with the woman in this poem?
4. How is the woman in "Virginia Portrait" similar to and different from Vyry in *Jubilee?*
5. **Literary Concept: Theme Theme** is the central idea that a writer wishes to share with a reader. Most themes are not stated directly but must be inferred. What do you think is the theme of this poem?

> ### CONSIDER
> ✓ the images of winter in the first stanza
> ✓ how the winter season relates to the woman
> ✓ what lesson or wisdom you can learn from the woman's life and character

Writing Prompt

Write a **dialogue** between Vyry in *Jubilee* and the woman in "Virginia Portrait" in which the two women describe their respective experiences and express their thoughts and philosophies about life.

You might want to distribute

 p. 34

from Incidents in the Life of a Slave Girl

Discussion Starters

1. How did you react to Dr. Flint's treatment of Linda, the name Harriet Jacobs uses for herself?

2. Why do you think Dr. Flint denies Linda's request to marry whom she pleases?

CONSIDER

✓ his relationship with her

✓ his response to her admission that she loves the man she wants to marry

✓ his attitudes toward the rights of those who are enslaved

3. If Linda were a friend who confided her troubles to you, what advice would you give to her?

4. Compare the experiences that Jacobs describes in this excerpt with Vyry's experiences while enslaved at Shady Oaks.

5. **Literary Concept: Point of View** This excerpt from Jacobs's slave narrative is told from the first-person point of view, as is most auto-biographical writing, whereas Walker's novel is told from an omni-scient third-person point of view. Which point of view, if either, has the greater impact on your reaction to what is being described? Explain your opinion.

Writing Prompt

Imagine you are a 19th-century abolitionist. Write an **antislavery pamphlet** in which you expose the evils of slavery. Draw on details in this excerpt from Jacobs's slave narrative as well as on your reading of *Jubilee*.

You might want to distribute

FYI *p. 35*

Raise a Ruckus Tonight
Many Thousand Gone

Discussion Starters

1. What thoughts or emotions came to mind as you read the lyrics to each of these songs?

2. In "Raise a Ruckus Tonight," Sara takes drastic measures to gain her freedom. Do you agree with her actions? Why or why not?

> ### CONSIDER
>
> ✓ the promises that her old master and mistress made to her
>
> ✓ the obstacles that Sara faces in obtaining her freedom
>
> ✓ the moral and legal implications of Sara's actions

3. In the second song, what do you think the repeated phrase "many thousand gone" refers to?

4. How do you think each of these songs might be sung—for example, fast or slow, or in a rousing or a mournful way?

5. Why do you think songs like these—and the ones quoted in *Jubilee*—were so important to the people who sang them?

Writing Prompt

"Many Thousand Gone" celebrates emancipation from slavery. The freeing of the enslaved people is represented by the different things they left behind when they were liberated, such as the auction block, their meager ration of corn, and the lash. Write additional **song lyrics** that could be added to this song, listing other things that slaves left behind. For ideas, use information about slavery that you have gleaned from *Jubilee* as well as from the related readings.

You might want to distribute

 p. 36

Come Up from the Fields Father

Discussion Starters

1. What image or images made the strongest impression on you as you read this poem?

2. Compare the mother's reaction to the letter from her son with the reactions of the other family members. How do you explain the difference?

3. Why do you think the speaker in the poem says that the son doesn't need to be better (line 29) but that the mother does (line 32)?

4. How are the mother's and Salina Dutton's responses to the deaths of their sons similar, and how are they different?

5. **Literary Concept: Irony** Irony refers to the heightened contrast between appearances and reality. In **situational irony,** events are structured so that what happens is usually the exact opposite from what is expected. Point out the irony in this poem, and explain the impact of this irony on your response.

CONSIDER

✓ the description of the physical surroundings in lines 3–11 and line 23

✓ the disruption that the letter causes

✓ the description of the mother in lines 24–25 and in the last stanza

✓ what the contrasts in the poem make you feel and think about

---

Writing Prompt

Emotional reactions to grief may include the following:

- emotional release such as crying
- depression and loneliness
- insomnia
- loss of appetite
- other physical symptoms
- panic
- guilt
- hostility and resentment
- dejection
- reconciliation
- adaptation

Write a brief **assessment** in which you analyze the mother's emotional state on the basis of the different reactions to grief that she exhibits in the poem.

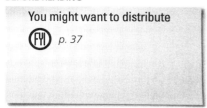

You might want to distribute

(FYI) *p. 37*

The Sheriff's Children

Discussion Starters

1. How did you react to the ending of the story?

2. Why do you think Tom decides to kill himself?

3. Do you think that Tom is guilty of Captain Walker's murder? Why or why not? Cite evidence from the story to support your opinion.

4. What do the sheriff's family relationships tell you about the connections between whites and blacks in the South?

CONSIDER

✓ the sheriff's struggles with his conscience

✓ his feelings toward his children

✓ his behavior in the past

✓ the irony of the outcome of the story

5. Compare and contrast the way Tom in the story and Vyry in *Jubilee* feel about their fathers.

Writing Prompt

Write a **newspaper article** for the *Branson County Banner* in which you report one of the following incidents: Captain Walker's murder, Sheriff Campbell's defense of Tom against a lynching party, Tom's attempt to escape from jail, or Tom's death in a prison cell.

Traveling the Long Road to Freedom

AFTER READING

Discussion Starters

1. What are your thoughts about Anthony Cohen's journey?
2. In your opinion, what was Cohen's biggest challenge in retracing a route on the Underground Railroad? Explain your opinion.
3. How would you characterize Cohen's emotional response when he finally reaches Canada?
4. According to Cohen, "You can only understand history so much from reading a book." Does he prove his point? Support your opinion with evidence from the selection.
5. How do you think Vyry in *Jubilee* might react to Cohen's project?

Writing Prompt

Write an **inscription** for a historical plaque that might be placed at the site of an Underground Railroad stop described in this article.

To the University of Cambridge, in New-England

Discussion Starters

1. What thoughts or feelings did you have after reading this poem?
2. **Literary Concept: Theme** Theme is the central idea the writer expresses. What do you think is Wheatley's main idea, or message, in this poem? Write a one-sentence summary.
3. Compare and contrast how the poem's speaker and Vyry in *Jubilee* feel about education.
4. **Making Connections** Wheatley wrote this poem in 1767 for Harvard University students, who at that time had a reputation for noisy, undisciplined behavior. Do you think the ideas expressed in her poem would be relevant to students today? Why or why not?

Writing Prompt

The speaker of this poem urges Harvard University students to make the most of their opportunities. Write a **list** of Do's and Don'ts for college students from the point of view of the speaker.

To Phillis Wheatley

Discussion Starters

1. In her response to Phillis Wheatley, Clayton includes information about Phillis Wheatley's life. What facts do you find most inspiring?
2. Why do you think Clayton identifies so strongly with Wheatley?
3. Margaret Walker drew on her grandmother's stories to write *Jubilee* and modeled Vyry on her great-grandmother. What questions do you think Clayton might want to ask Vyry, if she could?

Writing Prompt

Write a **fan letter** to a person who inspires you. You may want to write to a family member, a teacher, a friend, or a well-known person like Phillis Wheatley.

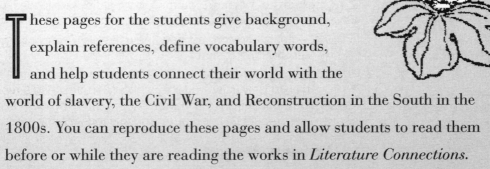

These pages for the students give background, explain references, define vocabulary words, and help students connect their world with the world of slavery, the Civil War, and Reconstruction in the South in the 1800s. You can reproduce these pages and allow students to read them before or while they are reading the works in *Literature Connections.*

Table of Contents

Jubilee

The Peculiar Institution

Slaves captured in Africa were first brought to the American colonies in the 1600s. By the 1800s, the system that many white Southerners came to call their "peculiar institution" (meaning something distinctive) was firmly rooted in the South. In all, about 20 million Africans were forced into slavery in America.

Slaves in the American South did not have rights. Considered property, they were bought and sold at their owners' discretion. They were not allowed to vote, legally marry, work for wages, hold their own religious services without white supervision, or travel without a pass provided by their masters. Furthermore, they had to endure a life of grueling poverty, backbreaking work, brutal living conditions, and heartbreaking separation from their loved ones.

The slaves typically lived in cramped slave quarters, consisting of one-room or two-room cabins with dirt floors, a stove or fireplace, windows without glass, and crude furnishings. They received periodic food rations and were allotted basic clothing items such as shoes, hats, and cotton shirts and pants. As a result of their difficult working and living conditions, slaves often suffered from diet-related diseases such as beriberi and pellagra as well as from contagious diseases such as lockjaw, typhoid fever, malaria, cholera, and dysentery.

Enslaved blacks drew strength from a distinctive African-American culture that emerged in slave quarters through the passing on of African beliefs and practices. As you learn by reading *Jubilee,* slaves spoke their own form of English, practiced herbal healing, and expressed their feelings in music and dance infused with African rhythms and patterns.

Get in the Spirit

Throughout *Jubilee,* Walker quotes lyrics from spirituals such as "Swing Low, Sweet Chariot" and "Rise Up, Shepherd." Spirituals are African-American religious folk songs that frequently follow the call-and-response pattern of African song. Improvised and transmitted orally by slaves, spirituals helped them deal with the situation of slavery. The lyrics of spirituals frequently include Biblical references that comment on enslavement and the hope of freedom indirectly, and some lyrics even incorporate secret messages that were to be sent from slave to slave. The well-known spiritual "Follow the Drinking Gourd," for example, was a musical map of one line in the Underground Railroad. Which spirituals that Walker quotes are you familiar with?

The History of the Story

Margaret Walker spent 30 years writing *Jubilee*. While she was in college, she wrote for a creative writing class 300 pages of a novel based on her grandmother's stories. After putting the novel aside for five years, she began conducting exhaustive research. Walker read countless history books, Civil War novels, and slave narratives. She diligently examined personal papers, diaries, newspaper articles, bills of sale, and letters, and listened to recordings of Civil War songs. Her research included trips to Georgia, where she learned more about her great-grandfather, the real Randall Ware, and the woman she calls Vyry. Walker saw the family Bible and a chest that her great-grandmother had taken with her when she left the plantation, as well as her great-grandfather's smithy, grist mill, and home. While raising a family, teaching, and working on a doctorate in English, Walker struggled to complete her novel. In her essay "How I Wrote *Jubilee,*" she recalls the moment she finally finished the first draft: "On the morning of April 9, 1965, at ten o'clock, I was typing the last words, "Come biddy, biddy, biddy, biddy/ Come chick, chick, chick, chick.'"

Chapters 1–18

PART I

Cotton Is King

In Part I, Walker describes life in the antebellum South. From the early 1800s to 1860, the economy of the South grew and prospered with a booming growth in cotton production. In response to a huge demand for cotton by the rapidly growing British textile industry, the South's cotton production skyrocketed, and by 1825 the South supplied most of the world's cotton. Large-scale cotton production created an enormous need for slave labor; consequently, planters like John Dutton bought more slaves to plant, cultivate, and harvest the crops.

Growth of Cotton Production and the Slave Population, 1790–1860

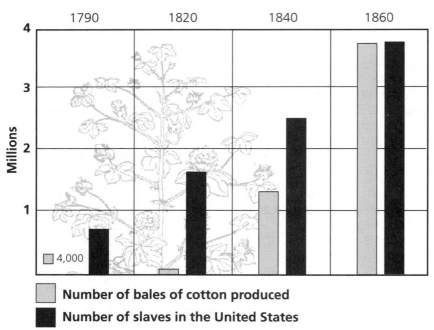

- ▢ Number of bales of cotton produced
- ▮ Number of slaves in the United States

Free Blacks

In the antebellum South, there were some African Americans who, for one reason or another, were not enslaved. Some had been set free by their masters; there were others whose freedom had been bought. Some were born free. Randall Ware was one of them.

Plantation Positions

Running a plantation like Shady Oaks was a daunting task. On many plantations, the work was divided among different people who performed specific jobs, as follows:

- **master** planter who owned the plantation and managed all of its business

- **mistress** planter's wife, who managed domestic affairs and took care of plantation business in her husband's absence

- **overseer** a white man who supervised groups of field slaves

- **driver** a privileged slave who helped the overseer supervise field slaves

- **artisan slaves** skilled blacksmiths, carpenters, spinners, weavers, and so forth

- **house slaves** slaves who did all the plantation's domestic work such as cleaning, cooking, washing, and waiting on the master and his family

- **field slaves** slaves who worked in the fields from sunup to sundown, laboring to plant, cultivate, and harvest crops such as cotton, rice, tobacco, and sugar

Chapters 1–18 (continued)

PART I

LITERARY CONCEPT

Allusion

An **allusion** is an indirect reference to a person, place, event, or literary work that the author believes the reader will be familiar with. In Chapter 10, Johnny Dutton compares his mother, Salina, to Spenser's Una. This is an allusion to the Elizabethan poet Edmund Spenser (1552?–1599) and to Una, the medieval heroine in Spenser's epic poem *The Faerie Queene.* As you read *Jubilee,* look for other allusions and discuss them with your classmates.

Jumping the Broom

Because Vyry and Randall Ware are not allowed to marry legally, they "jump the broom" in the presence of the black preacher, Brother Ezekiel (Chapter 14). This informal marriage ritual, which probably originated in Africa, involved literally jumping over a broomstick in the presence of other slaves or of the master or some other authority figure. Toward the end of the Civil War, white clergymen in the South who accompanied Union soldiers performed thousands of marriage ceremonies for couples who had "jumped the broom" in slavery but who desired to formalize their union in the eyes of God and the law.

LITERARY CONCEPT

Dialect

Hetta, Vyry, and other African-American characters introduced in Part I have a distinctive **dialect,** or way of speaking. The distinct form of the English language spoken by African Americans in the rural South is reflected in characteristic pronunciations, expressions, vocabulary, and grammatical constructions. To capture the way her African-American characters speak, Walker uses unconventional spellings such as those shown below.

Dialect Words	Conventional Words
footses	feet
gwine	going to
sho-nuff	sure
terreckly	directly
y'all	you all
needer	neither
Marster, Marse	Master

By pronouncing a dialect word as it is spelled and by looking at it in the context of the sentence, you can easily figure out the meaning of the word. The dialect in *Jubilee,* like the many quotations from folk songs and spirituals, not only lends authenticity to this historical story but also brings the characters to life.

VOCABULARY

Down South

In Part I, Walker uses words that were commonly used by whites and blacks in the South in the 1800s. Here are some examples.

clabber	sour, curdled milk
croker	sack; gunnysack
patter-rollers	whites who patrolled the countryside at night to make sure that slaves were in their houses or had the proper passes that allowed them to travel
pickaninny	disparaging term for a young African-American child
po buckra	poor white people
vittles	food

Chapters 19–40

PART II

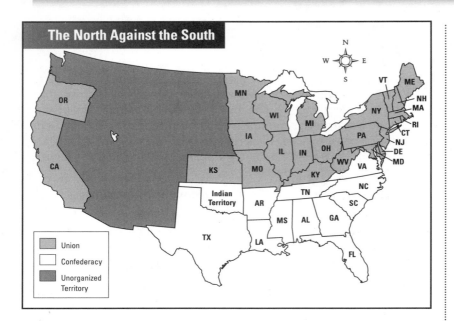

The North Against the South

Legend:
- Union
- Confederacy
- Unorganized Territory

You're in the Army Now

Military terms appear throughout Part II, which is set during the Civil War. Here are some examples.

battalion — a large body of organized troops

blockade — the isolation of a nation, an area, a city, or a harbor by hostile ships or forces in order to prevent the entrance and exit of traffic and commerce

brigade — a military unit consisting of a variable number of combat battalions

cavalry — combat troops trained to fight on horseback

furlough — a leave of absence or vacation, especially one granted to a member of the armed forces

infantry — units of combat troops trained to fight on foot

As you read Part II, look for other words related to the military in general and to the Civil War in particular.

Americans Versus Americans

In the 1860 presidential election campaign, candidates squared off on a key issue: slavery. The Republican candidate, Abraham Lincoln, opposed extending slavery into the territories. After Lincoln won the election, Southern states, viewing Lincoln as a threat to their economy and way of life, seceded from the Union and formed the Confederate States of America.

As tensions between the North and South mounted, Lincoln attempted to avoid war. On April 12, 1861, however, Confederate troops shelled the federal garrison at Fort Sumter in Charleston, South Carolina, forcing the federal troops to surrender. The most devastating war in U.S. history had begun. Fought on American soil from 1861 to 1865, the Civil War pitted brother against brother, friend against friend.

By the end of the war, both sides had suffered terrible losses. Approximately 620,000 soldiers had been killed. In the South, the cost of the war and the end of the plantation system resulted in skyrocketing inflation, high taxes, and serious food shortages. The South also suffered extensive physical damage. Although the battle-scarred landscape was soon repaired and restored, deep emotional scars caused by the war took longer to heal.

Chapters 19—40
(continued)

The Battle Hymn of the Republic

Part II of *Jubilee* takes its title— "Mine eyes have seen the Glory"—from the first line of "The Battle Hymn of the Republic," a poem written by poet and abolitionist Julia Ward Howe in 1861. After watching a review of Union troops, Howe was so moved that she later woke up in the middle of the night and in the dark quickly wrote down the words of her stirring poem. Published in the *Atlantic Monthly* in February 1862, the poem soon became a popular marching song of Union soldiers.

Taking Sides

The Duttons believe that the war will be over "by breakfast" and that the Confederacy will win. Study the chart at right, which compares Union and Confederate resources. Which side—the North or the South—actually had the advantages?

Who Was Who in the Civil War

Following are some of the following historical figures mentioned in the novel:

- **Abraham Lincoln** Illinois lawyer and politician who served as president of the United States from 1861 to 1865 and who was assassinated by John Wilkes Booth just five days after the Civil War ended

- **Ulysses S. Grant** United States Army officer who became the head of Union armies in 1864 after his victorious Vicksburg campaign

- **William T. Sherman** commander of the Union Army of the Tennessee, the Army of the Ohio, and the Army of the Cumberland who led his troops on a path of destruction from Atlanta, Georgia, to Savannah in 1864 and through South Carolina in 1865

- **Jefferson Davis** former United States Army officer and senator from Mississippi who resigned from Congress when Mississippi seceded and who subsequently became president of the Confederate States of America

- **Robert E. Lee** a Virginian who resigned from the United States Army in 1861 to lead Confederate forces and who became commander of the Army of Northern Virginia in 1862

- **Braxton Bragg** former Louisiana sugar planter who became a Confederate army officer and won a decisive victory at the Battle of Chickamauga in 1863

Comparison of Union and Confederate Resources at the start of the war		
	Union (23 States)	Confederacy (11 States)
Population	20,700,000	9,105,000 (including slaves)
Manufacturing establishments	110,000	18,000
Manufacturing workers	1,300,000	110,000
Miles of railroad	21,973	9,283
Estimated troop strength	2,100,000	850,000

Chapters 41—58

PART III

Reconstructing the Union

The events in Part III take place in 1866–1870, the early years of Reconstruction, when the United States struggled to rebuild itself after the Civil War. During Reconstruction (1865–1877), the federal government faced the tasks of readmitting Confederate states to the Union and determining the status of 4 million freed slaves like Vyry and Innis. The government created the Freedmen's Bureau to assist freed people and passed a significant number of laws to help the nation heal and move forward.

In the South, Reconstruction brought dramatic social, economic, and political change. Those who had been enslaved could now work for wages, marry legally, practice their religion freely, attend school, travel, and live together with their families. The men could vote and run for political office. The end of the plantation system gave rise to share-cropping and wage labor, and new state governments were established under Republican rule. As illustrated by the unfolding of events in Part III of the novel, such sweeping changes turned the lives of Southern blacks and whites upside down.

Share and Share Alike

In Chapter 44, Innis agrees to work for Mr. Pippins as a sharecropper. Sharecropping emerged during Reconstruction as an alternative to wage labor on plantations and to land redistribution. Plantation owners had land but no workers and no money to hire them; on the other hand, freed slaves and poor whites could work but had no land, tools, or money. To remedy this situation, landowners rented land to share-croppers and provided them with seed, tools, and other supplies in exchange for a share—usually one-half—of the harvest. Although this system held advantages for both parties, sharecroppers usually became trapped in a cycle of debt. By the time they shared their crops with landowners and paid their debts to local merchants, they had little or no money left.

Forty Acres and a Mule

In Chapter 44, Vyry and Innis discuss the government's promise to "give every colored farmer forty acres and a mule." Toward the end of the Civil War, thousands of freed slaves who had no land and nowhere to live followed Union troops across South Carolina. To solve this problem, General William T. Sherman issued Special Field Order No. 15 on January 16, 1865, giving freed slaves 40-acre plots in coastal Georgia and South Carolina and the loan of an Army mule. Some 40,000 freed African Americans settled on 400,000 acres of land that had been abandoned by Confederate planters. However, they were allowed to farm the land only for a short time before being forced to relinquish it to its original owners.

Chapters 41–58
(continued)

Law and Order

During Reconstruction, the federal government passed a series of acts and amendments to rebuild the nation and challenge the social and political order of the Old South. The chart below describes some of the landmark legislation and amendments that were passed during this period.

Reconstruction Legislation and Amendments

Legislation	Date	Purpose
13th Amendment	Ratified 1865	Abolished slavery in the United States
Freedman's Bureau	1865, 1866	Provided services for war refugees and freed people
Civil Rights Act	1866	Granted citizenship to African Americans
Reconstruction Acts	1867	Established Radical Reconstruction
14th Amendment	Ratified 1868	Guaranteed citizenship to all those born or naturalized in the United States and guaranteed due process and equal protection under the law
15th Amendment	Ratified 1870	Guaranteed voting rights for those of any race
Ku Klux Klan Act	1871	Sought to combat the Klan and similar organizations
Civil Rights Act	1875	Guaranteed African Americans equal rights in public places

Violent Vigilantes

In Chapter 46, the Ku Klux Klan terrorizes Vyry and her family by burning down their new house. Formed in 1866, the Ku Klux Klan was a secret organization that resorted to violence and intimidation to achieve its goals. The members of the Klan wanted to restore white supremacy, destroy the Republican Party, topple Reconstruction governments, and prevent blacks from exercising their political rights. Wearing white robes and hoods to disguise themselves, Klan members rode through the countryside at night, burning black schools and churches and attacking blacks and whites. Between 1868 and 1871, during the reign of terror waged by the Klan and other similar organizations, several thousand men, women, and children were killed. Such violence and harassment succeeded in turning African Americans away from polls and helped the South return to home rule by white Southern Democrats. Today, groups still exist that name themselves after the original Klan and promote aims of "white supremacy."

from Incidents in the Life of a Slave Girl

BY HARRIET A. JACOBS

Background

Harriet Jacobs was born into slavery in Edenton, North Carolina, in about 1813. Her first mistress, who taught her how to read, died when Jacobs was 11. Willed to 3-year-old Mary Matilda Norcrom, Jacobs went to live and work in the Norcrom household. As Jacobs describes in this excerpt from her book, she endured relentless sexual harassment at the hands of her mistress's father, Dr. James Norcrom. In 1835 Jacobs escaped from the Norcroms and went into hiding for almost seven years. Living in a tiny crawlspace in her grandmother's house, she passed the time writing, reading, and sewing. In 1842 she escaped to New York City and found a job working as a nursemaid for the Willis family. Although Dr. Norcrom made numerous trips to New York to try to catch her, Jacobs managed to elude capture. She faced the constant threat of being returned to slavery in the South until her employer, Cornelia Grinnell Willis, bought Jacobs for $300 in 1852.

For several years Jacobs lived in Rochester, New York, where she became active in the abolitionist movement. In March 1849 she began to work in an antislavery reading room, office, and bookstore that had been established by antislavery activists. Here she became acquainted with antislavery fiction, pamphlets, and slave narratives. At the urging of her white friend Amy Post, a Quaker reformer, Jacobs decided to write her autobiography in order to help the abolitionist cause. Her first published piece, "Letter from a Fugitive Slave," appeared anonymously in the *New York Tribune.* After trying to find a publisher for her book, Jacobs brought out *Incidents in the Life of a Slave Girl* on her own in 1861.

In Their Own Words

Incidents in the Life of a Slave Girl is a **slave narrative,** or a written account of slavery by a person who escaped or was freed from slavery. A uniquely American form of autobiography, slave narratives such as this one by Jacobs and *The Interesting Narrative of the Life of Olaudah Equiano* (1789) emerged as a persuasive tool for abolitionists in the years prior to the Civil War. Such deeply personal and harrowing first-hand accounts of slavery fueled public debate and drew attention to the antislavery cause.

Name Game

Harriet Jacobs intended to document her mistreatment and to persuade others to join the abolitionist movement by making her life's story public; however, she worried about how readers might react to her candid discussion of the sexual abuse of enslaved women and to her revelation that she had become involved with a white lawyer when she was a teenager and had two children by him. Jacobs thus initially published her slave narrative under a pseudonym, Linda Brent, and changed the names of important people in her account to keep their identities secret. In this excerpt, for example, she refers to Dr. James Norcrom and his son James Norcrom, Jr., as Dr. Flint and young Mr. Flint.

Jacobs's use of a pen name raised questions about the veracity of her account. In her preface to the 1861 edition of her book, she declared: "Reader, be assured this narrative is no fiction. I am aware that some of my adventures may seem incredible; but they are, nevertheless, strictly true. I have not exaggerated the wrongs inflicted by Slavery; on the contrary, my descriptions fall far short of the facts. I have concealed the names of places, and given persons fictitious names. I had no motive for secrecy on my own account, but I deemed it kind and considerate towards others to pursue this course."

Raise a Ruckus Tonight
Many Thousand Gone

The Birth of Spirituals

"Many Thousand Gone" is a spiritual that originated in the antebellum South and that was sung by African-American troops during the Civil War. In an address delivered in Philadelphia in 1862, abolitionist J. Miller McKim recounted a conversation he had had with an African-American soldier in the Union army. The soldier described the spontaneous, improvisational nature of spirituals in general, and this one in particular:

"I'll tell you: it's dis way. My master call me up an' order me a short peck of corn and a hundred lash. My friends see it and is sorry for me. When dey come to de praise meeting dat night, dey sing about it. Some's very good singers and know how; and dey work it in, work it in, you know, till dey get it right; and dat's de way."

Measuring Up

Some of the lyrics of "Many Thousand Gone" refer to slaves' rations, or fixed portions of food that enslaved people received weekly. A peck is a unit of dry volume equal to 8 quarts, and a pint, used in dry measure, is a unit of volume equal to 1/2 quart. Most of those enslaved felt that they received barely enough food to subsist on. To supplement their meager diets, they hunted, fished, raised vegetables in small garden plots, gathered nuts and berries, or stole from the master.

Sad Songs

In his autobiography, the formerly enslaved Frederick Douglass describes his emotional reaction to slave songs such as "Raise a Ruckus Tonight" and "Many Thousand Gone."

"They told a tale of woe which was then altogether beyond my feeble comprehension; they were tones loud, long, and deep; they breathed the prayer and complaint of souls boiling over with the bitterest anguish. Every tone was a testimony against slavery, and a prayer to God for deliverance from chains. The hearing of those wild notes always depressed my spirit, and filled me with ineffable sadness. I have frequently found myself in tears while hearing them."

VOCABULARY

What's All the Ruckus?

In "Raise a Ruckus Tonight," Sara plans to raise a ruckus—a disturbance or commotion—now that she is free. *Ruckus* is a portmanteau word, or a word formed by merging the sounds and meanings of two different words, here probably *ruction* and *rumpus*. The word *ruction* means "a riotous disturbance" or "noisy quarrel," and *rumpus* means "a noisy clamor." What other portmanteau words are you familiar with?

Come Up from the Fields Father

BY WALT WHITMAN

Background

Walt Whitman, one of America's most innovative and influential poets, was born on New York's Long Island in 1819. After attending school for five years, he went to work, at the age of 11, as an office boy. As a young man, he worked as a printer, a teacher, a journalist, and a carpenter. In 1848 he began to write free-verse poems for a single volume of poetry that became his life's work. In 1855, at his own expense, Whitman published a 12-poem book, *Leaves of Grass,* which he continued to revise and expand for more than 30 years. By the time the ninth and final edition was published in 1891, *Leaves of Grass* included almost 400 poems.

During the Civil War, Whitman traveled to the war front in Virginia after learning that his younger brother George had been wounded at Antietam. He remained in Washington, D.C., to work as a volunteer war nurse, giving out small gifts, changing dressings, comforting the sick, and entertaining soldiers with games and poems. Drawing on these experiences, he wrote Civil War poems such as "Come Up from the Fields Father," which appear in "Drum-Taps" and "Memories of President Lincoln," two sections in *Leaves of Grass.*

War Casualties

In this poem, parents in Ohio find out that their only son, Pete, has been injured while fighting in the Civil War. Tragically, Pete dies as a result of his wounds. The Civil War was America's bloodiest war, affecting almost every American family. As shown in the bar graph below, the war's human toll was staggering, especially considering that the population of the United States at the time was only about 31 million.

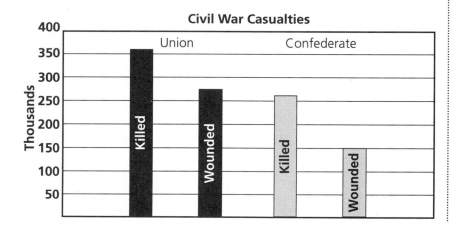

Civil War Casualties

Union — Killed, Wounded; Confederate — Killed, Wounded (Thousands: 50 to 400)

Free Verse

Walt Whitman is often credited with being the father of **free verse,** or poetry that does not have regular patterns of rhyme and meter. Even though free verse lacks regular meter and rhyme, it often contains other traditional elements of poetry. In this poem, for example, Whitman uses these traditional elements:

- **imagery** ("Smell you the smell of the grapes on the vines?")

- **repetition** ("But now from the fields <u>come</u> father, <u>come</u> at the daughter's call,")

- **alliteration** ("Smell you the <u>b</u>uckwheat where the <u>b</u>ees were lately <u>b</u>uzzing?")

- **assonance** ("Lo, where the tr<u>ee</u>s, d<u>ee</u>per gr<u>ee</u>n, yellower and redder,")

- **consonance** ("Where a<u>pp</u>les ri<u>p</u>e in the orchards hang and gra<u>p</u>es on the trellis'd vines,")

- **figurative language** ("sweeten Ohio's villages"; "All swims before her eyes,")

The Sheriff's Children

BY CHARLES WADDELL CHESNUTT

Background

Charles Waddell Chesnutt, the son of free African Americans and the grandson of a successful white tobacco merchant, was born in Cleveland, Ohio, in 1858. He grew up, during Reconstruction, in North Carolina, where he first became aware of the injustices of a caste system based on skin color, a theme that recurs in much of his fiction. While attending a school founded by the Freedmen's Bureau, Chesnutt studied Greek, French, and German and read literature by such authors as William Shakespeare, Alexandre Dumas, and Charles Dickens. When he was in his early 20s, he returned to Cleveland, hoping to establish himself as a writer.

Beginning with the publication of "The Goophered Grapevine" in 1887, Chesnutt received critical acclaim for a series of dialect stories that were firmly rooted in Southern folklore. Although his entertaining dialect stories were popular, he eventually decided to turn to more serious subjects. In his breakthrough short story, "The Sheriff's Children," and in later works such as *The Wife of His Youth and Other Stories of the Color Line* (1899), *The House Behind the Cedars* (1900), *The Marrow of Tradition* (1901), and *The Colonel's Dream* (1905), he tackled the theme of racial problems in the South after the Civil War. In 1928 Chesnutt was awarded the Spingarn Medal from the National Association for the Advancement of Colored People for his "pioneer work as a literary artist depicting the life and struggles of Americans of Negro descent."

LITERARY CONCEPT
Dialect

To capture the way whites and blacks in rural North Carolina spoke at the time, Chesnutt used characteristic pronunciations, expressions, vocabulary, and grammatical constructions.

Read these examples of **dialect** aloud to hear how Chesnutt's characters speak.

Unconventional Spelling	Conventional Spelling
ter	to
co'te	court
bairls	barrels
stidier	instead of
wuthless	worthless

As you read, find additional examples of dialect in "The Sheriff's Children." Then discuss with your classmates how Chesnutt's use of dialect helps establish the setting and flesh out the characters.

Mob Violence

In this story, an angry mob storms the Branson County jail, where Tom, the murder suspect, is being held. Intending to take justice into its own hands, the mob plans to lynch Tom, or illegally execute him without a trial. Lynchings peaked in the South after Reconstruction and continued into the 20th century. Between 1855 and 1900, more than 2,500 African Americans accused of crimes were shot, burned, or hanged without a trial. According to Alabama's Tuskegee Institute, the last recorded lynching occurred in 1964, bringing the total number of lynching victims in the United States since 1882 to 4,742.

Traveling the Long Road to Freedom

BY DONOVAN WEBSTER

Underground Railroad Routes

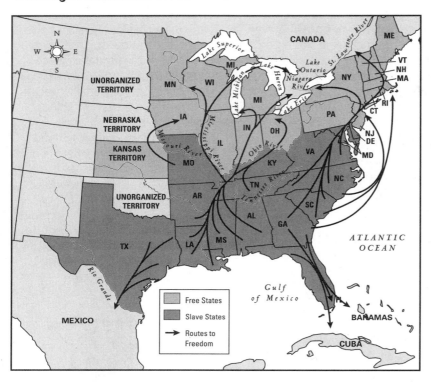

Free States
Slave States
→ Routes to Freedom

Profile: Harriet Tubman

Harriet Tubman (1820–1913) was born into slavery on a Maryland plantation. In 1849, after learning that she and her siblings might be sold, she escaped to Philadelphia. Instead of simply savoring her freedom, however, Tubman risked it to help other enslaved people. A leading Underground Railroad conductor, she made 19 hazardous trips to the South between 1850 and 1861 despite the fact that slaveholders had offered a $40,000 reward for her capture. Known as "Moses" because she led her people to freedom, she conducted about 300 slaves to freedom, including her own parents. In commenting on her heroic efforts, Tubman once modestly remarked: "I never run my train off the track, and I never lost a passenger."

Free at Last

As shown on this map, the Underground Railroad consisted of a complex network of escape routes from slave states in the South through free states in the North and into Canada. Brave "conductors" such as Harriet Tubman led people escaping from slavery out of the South, guiding them over the steep Appalachians and through mosquito- and snake-infested swamps. Traveling at night to avoid being caught, fugitives relied on the North Star and other natural signs to help them find their way. Once these people, known as "passengers," safely reached the North, "agents" escorted them from one "station" to another—usually a private home or a church—along the route. At Underground Railroad stations, free blacks and white abolitionists such as Levi Coffin and John Rankin provided hungry, exhausted passengers with food, shelter, and clothing.

Happy Juneteenth Day!

On January 1, 1863, President Abraham Lincoln issued the Emancipation Proclamation to abolish slavery in states "in rebellion." Soon after, Union armies marched throughout the South to read this proclamation aloud to groups of enslaved people. To this day, descendants of freed slaves around the United States celebrate "Juneteenth Day" to mark the date—June 19, 1863—when enslaved people in Texas first learned of their freedom. Anthony Cohen, during his journey, marches in a Juneteenth parade in Buffalo, New York.

Glossary

Part I: Chapters 1–18

admonition (ăd'mə-nĭsh'ən) *n.* cautionary advice or warning *p. 33*

amble (ăm'bəl) *v.* to walk slowly or leisurely; stroll *p. 21*

bondage* (bŏn'dĭj) *n.* the state of one who is bound in slavery *p. 49*

chagrin* (shə-grĭn') *n.* a keen feeling of mental unease, as of annoyance or embarrassment, caused by failure, disappointment, or a disconcerting event *p. 17*

cloying (kloi'ĭng) *adj.* causing distaste or disgust by supplying with too much of something originally pleasing, especially something rich or sweet *p. 4*

countenance (koun'tə-nəns) *v.* to give approval to; condone *p. 144*

demurely (dĭ-myoŏr'lē) *adv.* modestly; shyly *p. 10*

docile* (dŏs'əl) *adj.* yielding to supervision or management; obedient *p. 118*

exult (ĭg-zŭlt') *v.* to rejoice greatly *p. 139*

fetid* (fĕt'ĭd) *adj.* having an offensive odor *p. 8*

impudent* (ĭm'pyə-dənt) *adj.* characterized by offensive boldness; insolent or impertinent *p. 122*

insurrection (ĭn'sə-rĕk'shən) *n.* rebellion *p. 87*

patronizing* (pā'trə-nīz'ĭng) *adj.* condescending; dealing with in a superior manner *p. 156*

peevish (pē'vĭsh) *adj.* ill-tempered *p. 93*

petulant* (pĕch'ə-lənt) *adj.* unreasonably irritable; peevish *p. 93*

pious (pī'əs) *adj.* professing or exhibiting a strict, traditional sense of virtue and morality; high-minded *p. 10*

proscribed (prō-skrībd') *adj.* prohibited; forbidden **proscribe** *v. p. 100*

redress (rĭ-drĕs') *n.* satisfaction for wrong or injury; reparation *p. 101*

servile* (sûr'vəl) *adj.* of or relating to servitude or forced labor *p. 87*

taciturn* (tăs'ĭ-tûrn) *adj.* habitually untalkative; silent *p. 72*

tribulation (trĭb'yə-lā'shən) *n.* great affliction, trial, or distress; suffering *p. 14*

wizened (wĭz'ənd) *adj.* withered *p. 12*

Part II: Chapters 19–40

ameliorating (ə-mēl'yə-rāt'ĭng) *adj.* capable of making better or improving *p. 280*

annihilation* (ə-nī'ə-lā'shən) *n.* complete destruction *p. 294*

assent (ə-sĕnt') *n.* agreement *p. 274*

chafe (chāf) *v.* to feel irritated or impatient *p. 200*

destitute (dĕs'tĭ-toōt') *adj.* lacking resources or the means of subsistence; poor *p. 238*

diffident (dĭf'ĭ-dənt) *adj.* marked by a lack of self-confidence; shy and timid *p. 277*

emancipate* (ĭ-măn'sə-pāt') *v.* to free from bondage, oppression, or restraint *p. 216*

PARTIAL PRONUNCIATION KEY		
ă at, gas	îr dear, here	th thing, with
ā ape, day	ng sing, anger	*th* then, other
ä father, barn	ŏ odd, not	ŭ up, nut
âr fair, dare	ō open, road, grow	ûr fur, earn, bird, worm
ĕ egg, ten	ô awful, bought, horse	zh treasure, garage
ē evil, see, meal	oi coin, boy	ə awake, even, pencil,
hw white, everywhere	oŏ look, full	pilot, focus
ĭ inch, fit	oō root, glue, through	ər perform, letter
ī idle, my, tried	ou out, cow	

SOUNDS IN FOREIGN WORDS		
kh *German* ich, auch; *Scottish* loch	œ *French* feu, cœur; *German* schön	ü *French* utile, rue; *German* grün
n *French* entre, bon, fin		

* The words followed by asterisks are useful words that you might add to your vocabulary.

Glossary (continued)

impervious (ĭm-pûr'vē-əs) *adj.* incapable of being penetrated *p. 233*

impetuous* (ĭm-pĕch'ōō-əs) *adj.* impulsive and passionate *p. 280*

indelible (ĭn-dĕl'ə-bəl) *adj.* permanent *p. 311*

jubilation (jōō'bə-lā'shən) *n.* the act of rejoicing *p. 224*

malleable (măl'ē-ə-bəl) *adj.* capable of being shaped or formed *p. 295*

mollified* (mŏl'ə-fīd') *adj.* soothed; pacified **mollify** *v. p. 309*

piety* (pī'ĭ-tē) *n.* devotion and reverence to God *p. 204*

sanctimonious* (săngk'tə-mō'nē-əs) *adj.* feigning piety or righteousness *p. 204*

servitude (sûr'vĭ-tōōd') *n.* the state of subjection to an owner or master *p. 212*

subordination* (sə-bôr'dĭ-nā'shən) *n.* the state of being subject to the authority or control of another *p. 201*

suffuse* (sə-fyōōz') *v.* to spread through or over, as with liquid, color, or light *p. 276*

unctuous (ŭngk'chōō-əs) *adj.* characterized by affected, exaggerated, or insincere earnestness *p. 278*

vociferous* (vō-sĭf'ər-əs) *adj.* marked by noisy and vehement outcry *p. 199*

zealous* (zĕl'əs) *adj.* filled with or motivated by enthusiastic devotion to a cause, goal, or ideal; fervent *p. 192*

Part III: Chapters 41–58

abject* (ăb'jĕkt') *adj.* being of the most miserable kind; wretched *p. 412*

chastise* (chăs-tīz') *v.* to punish *p. 484*

congregated (kŏng'grĭ-gāt'ĭd) *adj.* gathered **congregate** *v. p. 396*

dissipated* (dĭs'ə-pāt'ĭd) *adj.* driven away; dispersed **dissipate** *v. p. 494*

dour (dŏŏr) *adj.* gloomy; glum *p. 435*

extricate (ĕk'strĭ-kāt') *v.* to release from an entanglement or difficulty *p. 341*

exude (ĭg-zōōd') *v.* to exhibit in abundance *p. 494*

halcyon (hăl'sē-ən) *adj.* calm and peaceful; tranquil *p. 477*

illiteracy (ĭ-lĭt'ər-ə-sē) *n.* the condition of being unable to read or write *p. 449*

impertinence* (ĭm-pûr'tn-əns) *n.* the quality or condition of being insolent, arrogant, or rude *p. 421*

infamy* (ĭn'fə-mē) *n.* disgrace *p. 451*

meager (mē'gər) *adj.* deficient in quantity; scant *p. 359*

resonant (rĕz'ə-nənt) *adj.* strong and deep in tone *p. 343*

respite (rĕs'pĭt) *n.* a usually short interval of rest or relief *p. 438*

sheepishly (shē'pĭsh-lē) *adv.* embarrassedly *p. 376*

strife (strīf) *n.* bitter conflict; discord *p. 489*

vilify* (vĭl'ə-fī) *v.* to make vicious and defamatory statements about; malign *p. 451*

---

* The words followed by asterisks are useful words that you might add to your vocabulary.

Name

Comparing and Contrasting

In Part I, Walker paints a vivid picture of life on a Georgia plantation in the 1800s. Slaves and slaveholders live side by side, yet their day-to-day lives are vastly different. To show the similarities and differences between the lives of Vyry and Lillian Dutton, complete the Venn diagram below.

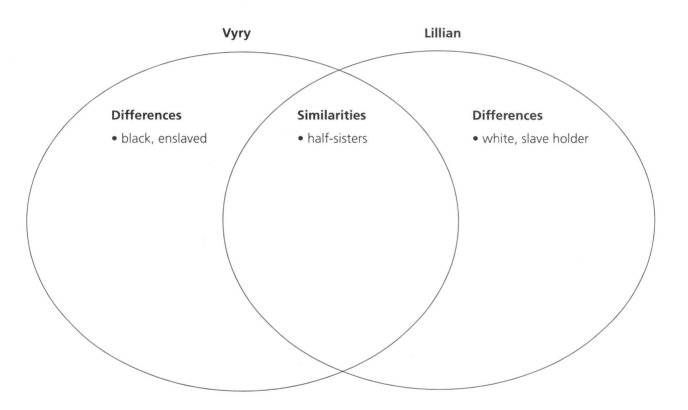

Vyry   **Lillian**

Differences
• black, enslaved

Similarities
• half-sisters

Differences
• white, slave holder

Identifying Cause and Effect

Events in novels are linked by cause and effect. The **cause** is the event that happens first in time and brings about what follows. The **effect** is what happens as a result of that first event. One effect can become the cause of another effect.

In *Jubilee,* the outbreak of the Civil War, in Chapter 22, causes a chain of events to take place. Complete the diagram below by listing five events that occur in the novel as a result of the outbreak of the war.

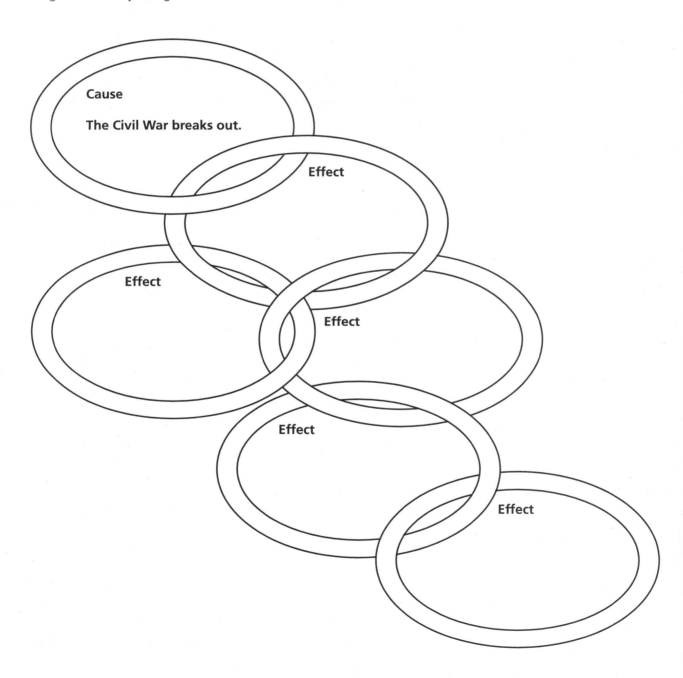

Identifying Problems and Solutions

In Part III, Vyry and her husband face a series of setbacks after they leave the plantation and try to find a home of their own. On the lines provided below, describe the problem the Browns face at each location. Then explain how they solve each problem.

The house in Alabama's low country

Problem/Solution

_____
_____
_____
_____
_____

Mr. Pippins's house

Problem/Solution

_____
_____
_____
_____
_____

The house in Troy

Problem/Solution

_____
_____
_____
_____
_____

Jubilee is a **historical novel** that is set during the period before, during, and after the Civil War. To tell her story, Walker weaves actual events and people together with fictional characters and events.

Complete the chart below by listing three events in *Jubilee* that actually occurred in history and three events that came from Walker's imagination. Then list the names of three people in the novel who actually lived and the names of three of the novel's fictional characters.

Historical Events	Fictional Events	Historical Figures	Fictional Characters
1.	1.	1.	1.
2.	2.	2.	2.
3.	3.	3.	3.

Name _____

In *Jubilee,* Walker uses **third-person omniscient point of view,** which means the following:

- The narrator is not a character in the story.

- The narrator presents the thoughts and feelings of various characters.

By using this narrative perspective, Walker helps us understand the thoughts and feelings of characters who have differing viewpoints: enslaved and free African Americans, abolitionists and slaveholders, Confederate soldiers and Union soldiers, wealthy landowners and poor farmers. Think about how this point of view helps shape the reader's reactions to the story and the characters and ties in with the author's purpose.

Complete the chart below. Indicate how much sympathy you feel as a reader toward each character. Then identify the group or element in society (for example, poor farmers) being represented by that character.

Character	Reader's feelings toward	Viewpoint represented
Vyry	___ Strong sympathy ___ Less sympathy ___ No sympathy	
John Dutton	___ Strong sympathy ___ Less sympathy ___ No sympathy	
Randall Ware	___ Strong sympathy ___ Less sympathy ___ No sympathy	
Innis Brown	___ Strong sympathy ___ Less sympathy ___ No sympathy	
Brother Ezekiel	___ Strong sympathy ___ Less sympathy ___ No sympathy	
Ed Grimes	___ Strong sympathy ___ Less sympathy ___ No sympathy	
Miss Lucy	___ Strong sympathy ___ Less sympathy ___ No sympathy	
Mrs. Jacobson	___ Strong sympathy ___ Less sympathy ___ No sympathy	

Literary Concept

STRUCTURE

The **structure** of a work of literature is the arrangement of its parts. *Jubilee* is divided into three parts, each covering a different historical period. Think about how this three-part structure gives coherence to a long and complicated series of events and how it shows characters being affected by history. Then complete the worksheet below. First, decide how you think the nature of each part of the book is suggested by its title. Second, list two or three of the most memorable events in each part. Third, briefly describe how Vyry grows or changes during each part.

	Part I. Sis Hetta's Child— The Ante-Bellum Years	Part II. "Mine eyes have seen the Glory"— The Civil War Years	Part III. "Forty years in the wilderness"— Reconstruction and Reaction
What title suggests			
Most memorable events			
Effects on Vyry			

Name _____

Review the asterisked words in the **Glossary** for *Jubilee*. Then complete the activities below.

A. Write *T* on the line if the statement is true. If the statement is false, change the sentence to make it true.

_____ **1.** **Fetid** odors in the kitchen make meals seem more appealing.

_____ **2.** **Impertinence** in a job interview improves your chances of success.

_____ **3.** **Abject** prison conditions are likely to result in calls for reform.

_____ **4.** Employees who are proud usually prefer a **servile** relationship to their boss.

_____ **5.** People are more likely to quarrel when their feelings have been **mollified.**

_____ **6.** It is necessary to **emancipate** offenders whose crimes are serious.

_____ **7.** The fog tends to be **dissipated** when the sun comes out.

_____ **8.** If you've been cheated, you may want to make a **vociferous** comment.

_____ **9.** If someone wants to **vilify** you, he might give you an honorary award.

_____ **10.** Doing a good deed often gives one a feeling of **infamy.**

_____ **11.** It is best to be **zealous** in the observance of safe driving rules.

_____ **12.** If you forget your lines in the school play, you will probably feel **chagrin.**

_____ **13.** It is wise to develop a **patronizing** attitude to one's friends.

_____ **14.** Lower-ranked soldiers are in **subordination** to higher-ranked ones.

_____ **15.** If light **suffuses** a room, you might want to open the curtains to let more sunshine in.

B. In each set of words below, circle the word that does not belong with the others.

1. servitude	bondage	emancipation	captivity
2. cross	irritable	docile	petulant
3. annihilation	extermination	creation	obliteration
4. cautious	impetuous	impulsive	rash
5. piety	irreverence	loyalty	devotion
6. congratulate	scold	chastise	reprimand
7. pious	impudent	sanctimonious	devout
8. disobedient	docile	tame	agreeable
9. reserved	taciturn	talkative	quiet
10. impertinent	impudent	courteous	insolent

Beyond the Literature

SYNTHESIZING IDEAS

Culminating Writing Assignments

EXPLORATORY WRITING

1. Think about the different experiences of African-American characters in *Jubilee* and in the related readings. Then write a newspaper **editorial** about racism, using the experiences of one or more of these characters as a springboard.

2. Write an **obituary** that might have been published in the *Macon Confederate and Telegraph* upon the death of one of these characters: John Morris Dutton, Salina Dutton, Johnny Dutton, or Kevin MacDougall.

3. Imagine that you are one of the characters in *Jubilee*. Write a **letter** to a friend about a significant event that you observed or experienced firsthand. You might describe, for example, the Fourth of July celebration (Chapter 11), the bloody Civil War battle at Chickamauga (Chapter 25), the reading of the Emancipation Proclamation by Union soldiers (Chapter 36), or the violent acts carried out by the Ku Klux Klan (Chapter 46).

RESEARCH

1. Find and read portions of a slave narrative such as *The Interesting Narrative of the Life of Olaudah Equiano* or *Narrative of the Life of Frederick Douglass*. Then write a **comparison and contrast essay** to examine similarities and differences between the slave narrative you read and either the fictional account of slavery in *Jubilee* or the excerpt from *Incidents in the Life of a Slave Girl*.

2. In Chapter 17, Vyry and her children attempt an escape from John Dutton's plantation by way of the Underground Railroad. Research the Underground Railroad and then write a **report** about how some enslaved people were conducted to freedom. As you research this topic, you may also want to draw on facts and details in "Traveling the Long Road to Freedom" (pp. 589–604).

LITERARY ANALYSIS

1. A writer usually writes for one or more of these purposes: to inform, to entertain, to express himself or herself, or to persuade readers to believe or do something. Write a **critical essay** in which you evaluate Walker's purpose in writing *Jubilee*.

2. Write a **comparison** between *Jubilee* and one of the related readings in this book. Compare the two pieces by focusing on a specific literary element, such as theme, character, conflict, imagery, or setting.

3. Choose one of the comments about *Jubilee* from the Critic's Corner pages provided by your teacher. Then write an **opinion essay** stating whether you agree with that critic. Support your views with evidence from the novel.

* For writing instruction in specific modes, have students use the **Writing Coach.**

Multimodal Activities

All in the Family

Have students draw a **family tree,** or genealogical diagram, of Vyry's family, including her parents, her siblings, her husbands, and her children. Display their diagrams by posting them on a bulletin board or by hanging them from a real tree branch in the classroom.

Stay Tuned

Ask students to imagine that a three-part miniseries based on *Jubilee* will soon be aired on television. Have them plan and create a one-minute **TV commercial** to advertise this upcoming miniseries. Suggest that they include music, a voice-over by a narrator who does not appear on camera, and images that depict the characters, the setting, and a sampling of the events that take place. Encourage students to videotape or perform their commercial for the class.

Plantation Plan

Have students draw a **diagram** of John Dutton's plantation, Shady Oaks, depicting the Big House, the Quarters, the cotton fields, the family cemetery, and other features mentioned in the novel. (This project can be tied in with the Cross-Curricular Project, Of Human Bondage, on page 53.)

Bon Appetit

As a young girl, Vyry is trained in the culinary arts. She eventually becomes the cook at the Big House. Students who enjoy cooking can prepare a **dish** that Walker mentions in *Jubilee* to share with the class. Suggest that they find recipes in a cookbook featuring traditional Southern cuisine. Encourage students to explain what ingredients they used and how the dish is prepared. (This project can be tied to the Cross-Curricular Project, What's Cookin', on page 54.)

Whose Side Are You On?

Have the class hold an **informal debate** or **discussion** as to how Reconstruction should have been handled. To do so, have students play the roles of characters in the last third of the novel, such as Vyry, Innis Brown, Randall Ware, Jim, Henry Turner (in the Georgia State House), old Doc, Mr. Pippins, Mr. or Mrs. Jacobson, Reverend Whittaker, Miss Lucy, Mr. or Mrs. Shackelford, and Mr. Porter. Students should prepare arguments based on their reading of the novel and the related readings as well as on their own research. Some students may wish to play the roles of historical figures not in the novel. Make sure the debate maintains a constructive tone and doesn't degenerate into emotional outbursts.

Drawing Battle Lines

Invite students to create a **map** on which they show the sites of key Civil War battles referred to in the novel, such as Vicksburg and Chickamauga, as well as the movement of armies and the progress of the war. Students may wish to add annotations to their maps in order to give more detail.

Gone But Not Forgotten

Remind students that a eulogy is a speech praising someone who has died. Ask students to plan and deliver a **eulogy** for one of the characters who dies in *Jubilee*.

Fashions of the Times

Have students research appropriate clothing styles of the mid-1800s, including the everyday dress of black women and white women, gowns that Southern women wore to balls and cotillions, and uniforms worn by Confederate and Union soldiers. Then ask them to sketch **costumes** that actors might wear in a filmed version of *Jubilee*. Display their sketches in the classroom.

Wilderness Wellness

In Chapter 9, Vyry gathers wild herbs and roots that she plans to eat or use for medicinal purposes. Invite students to research specific herbs and roots mentioned in *Jubilee* as well as those that grow in their own community. Have them create an illustrated **handbook** showing what the herb or root looks like and describing its various uses or healing properties. Caution students *not* to gather, taste, or experiment with samples of these plants.

From Dawn 'Til Dusk

Have students consider what a day in the life of an enslaved person was like based on their reading of *Jubilee* and the related readings. Have them create a **schedule** listing what chores a field slave like Innis Brown or a house slave like Vyry was typically expected to do either at certain times of the day or at certain times of the year.

Can You Carry a Tune?

Ask students to find and listen to recordings of popular Civil War **songs,** such as "Tenting on the Old Camp Ground," "The Bonnie Blue Flag," "The War Song of Dixie," or "The Old Union Wagon." Then have them analyze the lyrics and music. Guide them to discuss different aspects of war that the songs address as well as the emotions and views that the songs convey. You may also want to have students compare and contrast these songs with the spirituals and folk songs that are quoted throughout *Jubilee*.

Cross-Curricular Projects

The Sounds of Music

Overview:

Throughout *Jubilee,* Walker quotes lyrics from African-American spirituals. In this project, students will research the history of spirituals and locate the lyrics and music of a favorite spiritual. Students will conclude the project by presenting a brief oral report and by sharing a spiritual.

Cross-Curricular Connections: Music, Drama, History, Cultural Anthropology

Suggested Procedure:

1. Divide the class into small groups. Then have the members of each group work together to research spirituals. Suggest that they use an on-line or print encyclopedia, a dictionary of music, or a book about spirituals, or consult a music teacher or a musician who is familiar with spirituals, to find answers to the questions listed below.

- What are spirituals?
- When and where did spirituals originate?
- How are spirituals related to traditional African music?
- Why did people sing spirituals in the years around the Civil War?
- Why do people sing spirituals today?
- What kinds of emotions do spirituals express?
- What musical instruments, if any, are associated with spirituals?
- What are the titles of some well-known spirituals?

2. Encourage students to find the lyrics and music for a favorite spiritual, which may be one of those quoted in *Jubilee.* Tell them that they may locate either sheet music or a recording of the spiritual.

3. After groups finish their research, have them prepare oral reports. Ask them to plan to conclude their reports by performing or by playing a recording of their favorite spiritual. Have students who read music assist those classmates who plan to perform a spiritual from sheet music.

4. Have groups take turns presenting their oral reports. Beforehand, make sure that groups have any equipment they need—a record player, tape recorder, or CD player—to play recordings of spirituals.

5. After all of the groups have concluded their presentations, have students discuss why they think Walker incorporates lyrics from spirituals in her novel. Ask them: How do the spirituals quoted at the beginning of chapters capture the mood of the novel? How do the lyrics reflect what events take place? Also, have students identify and discuss lyrics from spirituals they have heard recently.

Teaching Tip

Remind students to speak slowly and clearly and to make eye contact when they give their oral reports.

Flora and Fauna of the South

Overview:

This project will give students an opportunity to learn more about the natural world in which *Jubilee* is set. After identifying and researching plants and animals that are indigenous to the South, students will create a bulletin board display based on what they have learned.

Cross-Curricular Connections: Biology, Botany, Geography, Social Studies, Art, Math

Suggested Procedure:

1. Divide the class into small groups. Have each group track down and list the names of specific animals and plants mentioned in *Jubilee* that are indigenous to the South. For example, students might list the following:

   - Spanish moss
   - bougainvillea
   - magnolias
   - whippoorwills
   - water moccasins (cottonmouths)
   - bobcats

2. Encourage groups to extend their lists by identifying other plants and animals that live in Southern states, such as camellias, palm trees, cypresses, and alligators.

3. Have groups research two or three plants and animals on their lists. Suggest that they locate information in a book about the South, a travel guide, a biology textbook, or a print or on-line encyclopedia.

4. Ask students to find representative pictures or photographs or create illustrations to show what the plants or animals they researched look like.

5. Have students write captions for their illustrations. Invite them to include information about where the plants and animals live, what their outstanding features or characteristics are, and whether they are considered endangered or threatened species. Also, suggest that they include, where appropriate, such vital statistics as height, weight, average lifespan, and so forth.

6. Ask groups to work together as a class to create a bulletin board display entitled *The Flora and Fauna of the South*. You might have them arrange their illustrations and captions on a map of Southern states. The map should make clear which species that were present in the 19th century are no longer present today.

Teaching Tip

You may want to invite an environmentalist, biologist, or botanist to speak to the class about specific plants and animals found in the South.

Of Human Bondage

Overview:

In this project, students will research different aspects of slavery to understand the context of *Jubilee.* They will research the transatlantic slave trade, plantation life, and the abolitionist movement. To present their findings, students will hold a symposium on slavery.

Cross-Curricular Connections: History, Geography, Art, Sociology, Economics, Math, Political Science, Government

Suggested Procedure:

1. Divide the class into three groups. Assign each group one of the following topics: the transatlantic slave trade, plantation life, or the abolitionist movement. Suggest that students use an American history textbook, a print or on-line encyclopedia, or a book about slavery to find information about their assigned topics.

2. Have the first group find answers to the following questions:
   - When and why did the slave trade in the Americas begin?
   - Who was involved in the slave trade?
   - How were slaves obtained, and where did they come from?
   - How were enslaved people transported to the Americas?
   - What was the "middle passage"?
   - How many people were brought to the Americas as slaves?
   - How did some African Americans happen to be free during this time?

3. Have the group researching plantation life find out how slaves lived, including what clothing they wore, what foods they ate, what jobs they performed, where they lived, how and why they were punished, and how they resisted enslavement. Suggest that students draw on factual information in *Jubilee* and in the related readings, in addition to the resources recommended in step 1.

4. Tell the last group to identify the goals of the abolitionist movement, its prominent leaders, how abolitionists spread their message, and whether the movement achieved its goals.

5. After groups finish their research, have them prepare for a symposium on slavery. A symposium is a meeting for discussion of a topic in which the participants form an audience and make presentations. Tell them that one or two students from each group will give a prepared talk on the topic their group researched. Urge them to create graphic aids such as maps, diagrams, time lines, and charts to enhance their presentations.

6. Have students hold the symposium. Allow speakers from each group to give their talks. Then, acting as the moderator, invite the audience to ask questions.

7. After the symposium, have students discuss what they learned about slavery and how the insights they have gained contribute to their understanding of *Jubilee.*

Teaching Tip

You may want to have students videotape their symposium to share with social studies classes.

What's Cookin'

Overview:

Historical novels incorporate accurate details that help readers picture a way of life in the past. To draw a realistic portrait of life in the South in the mid-1800s, Walker includes in *Jubilee* many details about food and food preparation. In this project, students will work independently to find recipes for dishes described in *Jubilee*. After locating recipes, students will work together as a class to create an illustrated cookbook.

Cross-Curricular Connections: Home Economics, Art, Math

Suggested Procedure:

1. Have students work independently to locate and list specific dishes mentioned in *Jubilee*. For example, they might list the following dishes:

   - fruitcake
   - roast pig
   - spoon bread
   - corn pone
   - watermelon rind conserve
   - hot mustard pickles
   - fried chicken
   - ginger cake
   - baked ham

2. Have students choose from the list one dish that they would like to prepare. Ask them to find a recipe for the dish in a cookbook. Have them write out the steps in chronological order, defining any unfamiliar terms or ingredients. Suggest that they use a personal computer and word processing software to type and print out a neat copy of the recipe.

3. As a class, students will share their recipes. Direct them to plan and create a class cookbook. Suggest that they arrange their recipes in alphabetical order; by type of dish, such as main dishes, side dishes, or desserts; or by key ingredients used to make the dish, such as chicken, eggs, or corn. Then have them place the recipes in a binder.

4. Encourage students to add a brief introduction to the cookbook as well as appropriate illustrations, a table of contents, and an index of recipes. Also, have them add a catchy title, such as *Vyry's Victuals* or *From Corn Pone to Possum*.

5. When students have finished the cookbook, you may want to make copies so that students can distribute them to friends, classmates, and family members.

> ### Teaching Tip
>
> Before students share their recipes, have them double-check the ingredients. They should test at least some of their recipes by cooking and eating the foods.

Suggestions for Assessment

Negotiated Rubrics

Negotiating rubrics for assessment with students allows them to know before they start an assignment what is required and how it will be judged, and gives them additional ownership of the final product. A popular method of negotiating rubrics is for the teacher and students respectively to list the qualities that the final product should contain, then compare the teacher-generated list with the student-generated list and together decide on a compromise.

Portfolio Building

Remind students that they have many choices of types of assignments to select for their portfolios. Among these are the following:

- Culminating Writing Assignments (page 48)
- Writing Prompts, found in the Discussion Starters
- Multimodal Activities (pages 49–50)
- Cross-Curricular Projects (pages 51–54)

Suggest that students use some of the following questions as criteria in selecting which pieces to include in their portfolios.

- Which shows my clearest thinking about the literature?
- Which is or could become most complete?
- Which shows a type of work not presently included in my portfolio?
- Which am I proudest of?

Remind students to reflect on the pieces they choose and to attach a note explaining why they included each and how they would evaluate it.

For suggestions on how to assess portfolios, see **Teacher's Guide to Assessment and Portfolio Use.**

Writing Assessment

The following can be made into formal assignments for evaluation:

- Culminating Writing Assignments (page 48)
- a written analysis of the Critic's Corner literary criticism
- fully developed Writing Prompts from the Discussion Starters

For rubrics to help you evaluate specific kinds of writing, see **The Guide to Writing Assessment** *in the* **Formal Assessment** *booklet of* **The Language of Literature.**

Test

The test on pages 56–57 consists of essay and short-answer questions. The answer key follows.

Alternative Assessment

For the kinds of authentic assessments found on many statewide and districtwide tests, see the **Alternative Assessment** booklet of **The Language of Literature.**.

Essay

Choose two of the following essay questions to answer on your own paper. (25 points each)

1. In *Jubilee,* Vyry lives through the antebellum years, the Civil War years, and some of the Reconstruction period that follows the war. What do you think are the most significant political, economic, and social changes that Vyry witnesses in each period—that is, in each of the three parts of the novel? To organize your thoughts, use a chart such as the one below, listing the events that you can think of in the categories to which they apply. Then write an essay pointing out what you think are the most important changes and why you think they are significant.

	Political Changes	**Economic Changes**	**Social Changes**
Part I			
Part II			
Part III			

2. Large Southern plantations like Shady Oaks were organized in a pyramidal hierarchy. From the owner at the top of the pyramid to the slaves at the bottom, each person who lived and worked on a plantation had a particular job to perform. Choose three major characters in *Jubilee.* Describe the various roles that each of these characters plays in plantation life, identifying where he or she fits into the plantation's pyramidal hierarchy.

3. Choose one of the following pairs to compare and contrast:

    a. Vyry and Harriet Jacobs in the excerpt from *Incidents in the Life of a Slave Girl*

    b. Salina Dutton and the mother in "Come Up from the Fields Father"

    c. John Dutton and Sheriff Campbell in "The Sheriff's Children"

4. Critic Bernard W. Bell views Vyry as a powerful and realistic "symbol of nineteenth-century black womanhood." What are Vyry's strengths and weaknesses? Why do you think Walker chose to build her story primarily around Vyry's experiences?

5. Imagine a sequel to *Jubilee.* What do you think will happen to Vyry and her children and Innis Brown? Consider what you know about the characters' lives thus far and how the novel ends.

Short Answer

On your paper, write a short answer for each question below and give a reason for your answer. (5 points each)

1. How might Vyry's life have been different if she had not been born into slavery?

2. Why do you think John Morris Dutton upholds slavery?

3. In a sentence or two, summarize what the antebellum years were like for whites and for blacks in the South.

4. How would you describe the fate of the Dutton family—Salina and her children, Johnny and Lillian—during the Civil War?

5. What are some words you would use to describe the Civil War years in the South based on your reading of *Jubilee?*

6. How does life at Shady Oaks change after the Civil War?

7. Think of an adjective that describes the Reconstruction years in the South, and give a reason for your choice.

8. What do you think is the most important decision Vyry makes after her reunion with Randall Ware? Explain.

9. What role does music play in the lives of African-American characters in *Jubilee?*

10. Why does Vyry feel "peace in her heart" at the end of the novel?

Test Answer Key

Essay

Answers to essay questions will vary, but opinions should be stated clearly and supported by details from the text. Suggestions for points to look for are given below.

1. Political changes include Lincoln's issuance of the Emancipation Proclamation; the passage of the Thirteenth Amendment, abolishing slavery; the South's defeat in the Civil War; the election of President Ulysses S. Grant; and the granting of African-American suffrage. Economic changes include the collapse of the plantation system, the growth of tenant farming or sharecropping, and the opportunity for freed African Americans to work for wages. Social changes for African Americans include being freed, gaining the right to legally marry, owning a home, and being victimized by members of the Ku Klux Klan.

2. Students may choose any three characters. For example, they may explain that John Dutton, the owner of Shady Oaks, is at the top of the pyramid. His job is to hire an overseer, to house and feed the slaves, to purchase and maintain farming equipment, and to deal with all of the financial matters related to the plantation. Ed Grimes, the overseer, is in the middle. His job is to supervise the slaves and make sure that they do their work properly. At the bottom are field hands like Innis Brown. His job is to pick crops such as cotton and tobacco.

3. **a.** Like Vyry, Harriet Jacobs was a house slave. Both women fell in love with free-born men who were artisans; their requests to marry these men were denied. Vyry worked for her white father, a planter, on a Southern plantation, Jacobs worked for a white doctor in a town.

   b. The only sons of both Salina and the mother in the poem are killed in the Civil War. Salina, the wife of a wealthy Southern planter, lives on a plantation in Georgia. Her son Johnny is shot in the lung and returns home to die. In contrast, the mother in the poem is married to an Ohio farmer. After being shot in the chest, her son, Pete, is taken to a hospital, where he dies.

   c. Both John Dutton and Sheriff Campbell are educated men from wealthy Southern families. Both pursue politics: Dutton in the Georgia legislature, and Campbell as a sheriff in North Carolina. Both fathered children by slaves they owned. Although the sheriff initially opposed secession and supported the Union in the Civil War, he later served in the Confederate army. Unlike the sheriff, Dutton died before the war began.

4. Vyry's strengths are her deep religious faith, skills in cooking and singing, loyalty to others, dignity, courage in surviving hardships of slavery, lack of bitterness or rancor, and practical nature. Vyry's weaknesses are political naiveté, relative complacency in accepting her fate, and sense of duty to the Duttons.

   Perhaps Walker built the story around Vyry because it was primarily her great-grandmother's story that she wanted to tell. Or, Walker made this choice because Vyry is uniquely situated to give readers a realistic look at what life was like for slaves in the South. A strong, capable African-American woman, a house slave, Vyry has a front-row seat to emancipation, the Civil War, and Reconstruction.

5. The Browns may continue to live in Alabama, farm the land, and work hard to improve their lives. Jim may become either a teacher or a minister and Minna and her younger siblings may attend school. Or the Brown family may again be forced to move from their home, facing more prejudice and discrimination following Reconstruction. Vyry may change her mind about staying with her husband and may renew her relationship with Randall Ware.

Short Answer

Answers will vary but should reflect the following ideas.

1. She might have been educated, lived with Ware in their own home, moved about freely, practiced her religion openly. As the daughter of a black mother and a white father, however, Vyry would still have faced prejudice.

2. A product of his environment, Dutton has been shaped by traditional Southern culture and values, and firmly believes that slavery is an economic necessity because the South's agricultural system depends on it. Like his father before him, he also believes that African Americans are better off enslaved.

3. For whites, the antebellum years were productive, tranquil, and bounteous. Blacks experienced oppression, discrimination, cruelty, and deprivation.

4. Salina, a widow, runs the plantation by herself, loses her only son, suffers a massive stroke, and dies. Johnny enlists in the Confederate army, is shot in the lung at the Battle of Chickamauga, is brought home by a loyal slave named Jim, and slowly bleeds to death. Lillian's husband, Kevin, suffers a bayonet wound at Olustee, and comes home to die. Widowed and left alone at Shady Oaks, Lillian is savagely attacked by Union soldiers. Although she physically recovers from the attack, she loses her mind.

5. Turbulent, anxious, violent, dangerous, brutal, unsettling, frightening, desperate. For many, the war years meant grief, hard work, deprivation.

6. No longer bustling and prosperous, Shady Oaks is nearly abandoned; crops are grown only to feed the few still living there. Jim, May Liza, and Caline leave with the soldiers who come to read the Emancipation Proclamation. Although free to go, Vyry stays on for a year, to wait for Randall Ware and to care for Lillian and Lillian's children. Once Lillian's aunt arrives to take Lillian away, Vyry consents to marry Innis Brown and leaves Shady Oaks for good.

7. Possible adjectives include: *confusing, bewildering, promising, exciting, daunting, uncertain, frustrating, disappointing, heartbreaking, intimidating.*

8. She decides to stay in Alabama with Innis Brown to raise their son Harry, the new baby that they are expecting, and her daughter by Randall Ware, Minna.

9. These characters sing songs, especially spirituals, to help them cope with tragedy and sorrow, to express themselves, to protest their condition, to lift their spirits, to pass the time, and to commemorate events such as death.

10. It is because she is finally free to live her life as she chooses. Reunited with Randall Ware, she realizes they do not have a future together. Contented with her life with Innis in her new home, she has lived to see her dream fulfilled.

Additional Resources

Other Works by Margaret Walker

For My People. 1942.
This book of poems, which celebrates African-American culture, won the Yale Series of Younger Poets Award in 1942.

Prophets for a New Day. 1970.
A collection of poetry that celebrates the civil rights movement of the 1960s and its leaders, including Malcolm X and Martin Luther King, Jr.

Richard Wright: Daemonic Genius. 1988.
A biography of Richard Wright, the acclaimed author of *Black Boy* and *Native Son*.

This Is My Century: New and Collected Poems. 1989.
In this collection of poems, Walker passes on her thoughts and feelings about racism and about her identity as an African-American woman.

How I Wrote Jubilee *and Other Essays on Life and Literature.*
1990.
This collection of essays includes "How I Wrote *Jubilee,*" which details the genesis of Walker's first novel.

FICTION and DRAMA

Beach, Lewis. *The Clod.* New York: Samuel French, 1914. Set during the Civil War, this one-act play describes how poor white farmers Mary and Thaddeus Trask are reluctantly drawn into the conflict. **(average)**

Bierce, Ambrose. "An Occurrence at Owl Creek Bridge." *The Complete Short Stories of Ambrose Bierce.* Garden City, NY: Doubleday, 1970. This haunting story traces the fate of Peyton Farquhar, an Alabama planter, during the Civil War. **(average)**

Mitchell, Margaret. *Gone with the Wind.* New York: Macmillan, 1939. Set in Georgia at the time of the Civil War, this historical novel tells the story of Scarlett O'Hara, a woman who lives through the war and watches as her plantation, Tara, is burned by General William T. Sherman's troops. **(average)**

Stowe, Harriet Beecher. *Uncle Tom's Cabin.* New York: Modern Library, 1985. The brutality of this classic novel, which was first published in 1852, shocked readers. The main character, Uncle Tom, endures life as an enslaved person. He is eventually beaten to death as a result of the orders given by a white plantation owner from the North, Simon Legree. **(average)**

POETRY

Hudgins, Andrew. *After the Lost War: A Narrative*. Boston: Houghton Mifflin, 1988. This sequence of poems is based on the life of Sidney Lanier, a poet and musician from Georgia who fought for the Confederacy in the Civil War. **(average)**

Whitman, Walt. *Leaves of Grass*. New York: Vintage Books/The Library of America Edition, 1992. Poems in the sections entitled "Drum-Taps" and "Memories of President Lincoln"—including "Cavalry Crossing a Ford," "When Lilacs Last in the Dooryard Bloom'd," "O Captain! My Captain!", and "Beat! Beat! Drums!"— deal with the Civil War. **(average)**

NONFICTION

Douglass, Frederick. *Narrative of the Life of Frederick Douglass, an American Slave*. New York: Anchor Books, 1989. In this remarkable autobiography, Douglass describes his experiences as an enslaved person and how he strove to become free. **(challenge)**

Haley, Alex. *Roots: The Saga of an American Family*. Garden City, NY: Doubleday, 1974. The author traces his origins back several generations to Kunta Kinte, a 17-year-old boy who was kidnapped in Gambia, enslaved, and brought to the United States. **(challenge)**

Lester, Julius. *To Be a Slave*. New York: Dell, 1968. In this work of nonfiction, Lester draws on slave narratives to create a history of slavery in the United States. **(average)**

Lincoln, Abraham. "The Gettysburg Address." Lincoln delivered this speech at the dedication of a cemetery at the Gettysburg, Pennsylvania, battlefield where more than 50,000 Union and Confederate soldiers were killed, wounded, or missing in the Battle of Gettysburg during the Civil War. **(average)**

Murphy, Jim. *The Boys' War*. Boston: Clarion Books/Houghton Mifflin, 1990. This is an account of the Civil War as seen through the eyes of the teenaged boys who fought in the Union and Confederate armies. **(easy)**

Truth, Sojourner. "Ain't I a Woman?" Sojourner Truth, an illiterate freed slave, gave this speech at a women's rights convention in Akron, Ohio, in 1851. **(average)**

MULTIMEDIA

The Civil War: A Film by Ken Burns. Video recording. PBS Home Video, distributed by Pacific Arts Video Publishing, 1991. Produced by Ken Burns. This award-winning documentary series, which originally aired on PBS, brings to life the events of the Civil War through photographs, excerpts from letters and diaries, and artifacts. 9 videotapes. 11 hrs. 20 min. **(videocassettes)**

A Firebell in the Night. Video recording. New York: Time-Life Video, distributed by Cine Magnetics Film and Video, 1972. Directed by Michael Gill. This BBC TV co-production with Time-Life Films, written and narrated by Alistair Cooke, discusses the causes and effects of the Civil War and the racial discord that still exists in the United States today. 51 min. **(videocassette)**

Glory. Video recording. Hollywood: Tri-Star Pictures, released by RCA/Columbia Pictures Home Video, 1989. Directed by Edward Zwick. Denzel Washington, Morgan Freeman, and Matthew Broderick star in this film about African Americans who fought in the Civil War in the 54th Massachusetts Infantry. 122 min. **(videocassette)**

Interview with Margaret Walker. Sound recording. Columbia, Mo.: American Audio Prose Library. An interview with Walker in which she discusses African-American literature and her writing of *Jubilee.* 86 min. **(audiocassette)**

Margaret Walker Reads Jubilee. Sound recording. Columbia, Mo.: American Audio Prose Library. Walker reads excerpts from *Jubilee,* including scenes from Vyry's childhood, Chapters 11 and 48, and selections from the final pages of the novel. 2 cassettes. 108 min. **(audiocassettes)**

An Occurrence at Owl Creek Bridge. 16mm film. New York: McGraw-Hill, 1962. The film version of Bierce's classic story of a man condemned to hang for sabotage during the Civil War. 29 min. **(film)**

Roots. Video recording. Wolper Productions, distributed by Warner Home Video, 1981. Produced by Stan Margolies. Directed by Marvin Chomsky, David Green, and John Erman. The filmed version of the book by Alex Haley. 6 videotapes. 9 hrs. **(videocassettes)**

Win a *Free* Classroom Set of Literature Connections!

FROM
⚜ McDougal Littell

Join the growing community of educators who are using *Literature Connections* to teach the novels and plays they want to teach, each supplemented by additional readings bound together in one hardbound book.

Simply complete and return this postage-paid questionnaire card and you're automatically entered into the McDougal Littell drawing to win a free classroom set of the *Literature Connections* titles of your choice!

LITERATURE CONNECTIONS

YES! Please enter me in the McDougal Littell Literature Connections drawing!

NAME_____

SCHOOL_____ POSITION_____

SCHOOL ADDRESS_____ CITY_____ STATE_____ ZIP_____

COUNTY_____ SCHOOL DISTRICT/DIOCESE_____

COURSES TAUGHT_____

_____

WHAT NOVEL(S) OR PLAY(S) DO YOU TEACH?_____

ARE YOU USING LITERATURE CONNECTIONS IN YOUR CLASSES?   YES____   NO____

WOULD YOU LIKE TO BE INVOLVED IN FUTURE RESEARCH OR PRODUCT DEVELOPMENT? YES____ NO____

PHONE NUMBER: SCHOOL (_____)_____ HOME (_____)_____

FREE PERIOD_____

⚜ **McDougal Littell** Information: 800-323-5435
International fax: 847-424-3433
Internet Address: http://www.mcdougallittell.com

P40166
1100.013

PC103